Acclaim for M A R I O N   W I N I K ' S

TELLING

"Details the joy of confession.... Winik is the mistress of the pithy sentence, delivering plenty of information per word."
—*Washington Post Book World*

"I love the book. It's great. Buy it and read it."
—Suzy Banks, *Austin Chronicle*

"Winik has undergone a prodigious metamorphosis on the road to maturity. Her reflections on the way she was and what she has become are nothing if not frank. She sets them down to amuse us and make us think."
—*Boston Sunday Globe*

"Winik has done all the things our parents warned us about, and she's gone on to write about them with astonishing candor, clarity and good humor."
—*Dallas Morning News*

"Hilarious, revealing and often poignant. Winik's electric wit informs it all."
—*Austin-American Statesman*

"Winik shares her wild romp from the '60s to the '90s in a series of hilarious reflections. Winik's light look at heavy issues now... covers everything from sibling rivalry to AIDS, from loss of a pet to psychedelic drugs; she pokes around in your memories and challenges current opinion as she shares hers.... A wise lady."
—*Indianapolis News*

"Poignant...controversial. Winik [has a] mesmerizing ability to evoke humiliation, humor and affection all in one paragraph."
—*Texas Monthly*

MARION WINIK

TELLING

Marion Winik's personal essays are heard regularly on National Public Radio's *All Things Considered* and appear in periodicals ranging from *Parenting* to *Playgirl* to *The Utne Reader*. She lives in Austin, Texas, with her two sons.

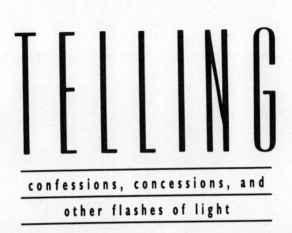

TELLING

confessions, concessions, and
other flashes of light

MARION WINIK

VINTAGE BOOKS

A Division of Random House, Inc.

New York

For Hayes Anthony Winik and Vincent Valdric Winik,
please wait until you are at least fourteen to read this book,
and in memory of Steven Cerbo

FIRST VINTAGE BOOKS EDITION, FEBRUARY 1995

Copyright © 1994 by Marion Winik

All rights reserved under International and Pan-American Copyright
Conventions. Published in the United States by Vintage Books,
a division of Random House, Inc., New York, and simultaneously
in Canada by Random House of Canada Limited, Toronto.
First published in hardcover by Villard Books, a division of
Random House, Inc., New York, in 1994.

These essays have been previously published, some in different form, in
American Way, The Austin Chronicle, The Houston Chronicle,
Parenting, and Texas Monthly.

The Library of Congress has cataloged the Villard edition
as follows:
Winik, Marion.
Telling: confessions, concessions, and other flashes of light /
Marion Winik.
p.   cm.
ISBN 0-679-42859-3
1. Baby boom generation—United States.   2. Maturation
(Psychology)   I. Title.
HN65.W54   1993
30524—dc20   93-6322
Vintage ISBN: 0-679-75522-5

Manufactured in the United States of America
10 9 8 7 6 5 4 3 2 1

Acknowledgments

Many thanks to Louis Black at *The Austin Chronicle*, who published early versions of several of these pieces; to John Burnet, who read them in the *Chronicle* and asked if I would record a demo tape for National Public Radio; to Margaret Low Smith at *All Things Considered*, who liked the tape and encouraged me to do more; to Patricia Van der Leun, who heard me on the radio, wrote to ask if there was a book, and helped me see that the answer was yes; and to Diane Reverand at Villard, who agreed.

For their intelligent, honest criticism and Tuesday-night camaraderie, thanks to the women in my writing group: Robin Bradford, Jerri Kunz, Miriam Kuznets, Martha Boethel, Jane Thurmond, Amy Smith, Karol McMahan, and Judith Ferguson.

For their thoughtful readings of the manuscript, deep

curtsies to my writer friends Naomi Shihab Nye and Robert Draper. For good advice on touchy subjects, thanks to Kathy Korniloff.

For their Fellowship in Literature, which bought me some time to write, amazement and gratitude to the National Endowment for the Arts.

My greatest debt, though, is to the family and friends who have put up with me all these years, and whose stories these are as much as they are mine.

MARION WINIK
AUSTIN, TEXAS
JUNE 1993

Contents

TELLING

Telling

ast summer I snapped the tip off my friend Anita's new ninety-dollar chef's knife by using it to try to pry open a tin of Japanese horseradish. A triangle of metal flew into the mysterious void where small shiny things sometimes go.

I stared at the huge gleaming broken knife in my hand and went into some kind of weird sociopathic state. I walked over to the sink, plunged the knife into the suds, pulled it out, and exclaimed, Oh God, look what happened to the knife. It must have broken somehow in the sink.

Anita looked at me in a funny way, and then everyone rushed over to see what was going on. Don't worry, Anita, they said, surely the store will replace it. A knife like that should stand up to a little use! You barely even had it one whole day.

If they don't, I said, I'll buy you a new one.

Why? asked Anita.

Oh, I just feel bad about it, I said.

Why? asked Anita. It's not your fault.

I guess not, I said in my weird sociopathic voice.

I had a lousy time that night, then went home and suffered some more. As soon as I got up the next morning, disasters began to befall me with alacrity. I sprained my ankle, misplaced a savings bond, and spilled coffee grounds all over the kitchen. I knew it was just my bad karma for telling such a big honker lie to my friend and then sitting down at her dinner table with that lie between us like a dead fish on a platter with its yellow eyes staring.

The next morning, I couldn't stand it anymore. I called Anita and told her the truth, which she of course had known all along. You are so silly, she said, and we both laughed, I perhaps more nervously than she. When I got off the phone, my ankle was miraculously healed and I found the savings bond right underneath my nose.

It was the perfect confession experience. I was off the hook, so to speak, precipitately pardoned and paroled, transformed from a bad person to a good person, just like that. My despicable crime had become a funny story, which I repeated to anyone who would listen.

I'm not claiming to be truly honest. If I were, I wouldn't have lied to Anita about the knife in the first place. There's a difference between being honest and telling. Where honesty is pure, telling expects results. At the very least, a bond between the teller and the tellee. At best, the big stuff: amnesty, redemption, grace.

As a child, I was jealous of Catholics, who had a beautiful lady in a blue robe to watch over them and forgive them, no matter what. In my own religion, God did not have a mother or a girlfriend or female representatives on earth. Every girl in the Hebrew school pageant had to be Queen Esther or a pillar of salt.

When I did my friend Carolyn Mahoney's catechism homework for her, I was amazed. Saints, angels, babies in limbo, medals that could protect you against things: was this a religion or a sideshow? What about this confession thing? Did they really go into a little booth, get down on their knees, describe their sins to a disembodied voice (Pay no attention to the man behind the curtain!), say a few prayers, and come out clean?

Just in case, I memorized the words to Hail Mary. I would say them over and over until the humming went straight down into my soul. But Hail Mary or no, I was not a Catholic. So who was going to give me absolution for trying to have sex with my cat?

If I couldn't be redeemed, I could perhaps at least be understood or loved. To this end, I always found a special moment to confess to new acquaintances that I had tried to commit suicide when I was twelve. Not only did I feel that this explained my entire personality but I also imagined it would bind my new friend to me inextricably, for life. If only out of fear that I would kill myself otherwise.

Unfortunately, the Awful Secret approach to interpersonal relationships often fell short of producing the desired result. For example, back in grade school, I was a compulsive wiggler. This was my word for it at the time. Every night in bed with my tattered stuffed bunny rabbit underneath me, I wiggled like a maniac. I couldn't stop. The headboard of my bed banged against the wall, my sister across the room couldn't get any sleep, and my mother would come in and say, Jesus Christ, stop that now! The bunny's ears fell off from all the abuse. One day I stayed after school to confess my problem to my beautiful blond-haired fifth-grade teacher, Miss Daly, perhaps confusing her with the Blessed Virgin. Her reaction, however, was distant and embarrassed: she suggested I see the school psychiatrist. Didn't she understand that I wanted to bond with *her*, not some strange man with a beard? I was glad when she left our school before the end of the year.

Years later, three high school friends of mine plotted and carried out the robbery of a convenience store. One of them was Alan Jacobson, infamous homecoming parade float coordinator. No matter what had happened between us, I was still in love with Alan; no matter what had happened between us, he still didn't love me. So I phoned in an anonymous tip to the police, and the robbers got caught. Part of it was that I couldn't keep a secret, part of it was revenge, but mostly, I believe, it was that I thought if he was in trouble he would need me more. When that didn't work, I took the next logical step—I confessed to him what I had done.

Though you may think it unsurprising that this, too, failed to win me his adoration, it was a great blow to me at the time.

As a child, I subscribed to a magazine titled *Calling All Girls*. One of my favorite parts of the publication was the department called "Was My Face Red!," which featured descriptions of embarrassing experiences contributed by humiliated readers.

I wrote to this column frequently, though my letters were never printed. I described the time I had walked in on another little girl sitting on the toilet in the basement lavatory of Wanamassa School. The green cinderblock walls, the light filtering through the casement window, the thin wooden door of the stall, the white anklets in their black Mary Janes dangling inches off the floor. I never even saw her face. Was it as red as mine? In another letter, I chronicled the mortification I had suffered the time my mother chaperoned our class trip to the Franklin Museum in Philadelphia. As we waited on line to get in, she spit on her finger to wipe a smudge off my cheek with the entire fifth grade watching. My skin turned rosy as she touched it.

By my preteen years I had realized you could tell

virtually anything to anyone if you put it in literary form. Forget *Calling All Girls*; I started my career as a poet right away. My primary themes included suicide, depression, insanity, unrequited love, the insignificance of human life, the cruelty of nature, and the Vietnam War. For my pen name, I chose Tracy Beth Richardson. My father had his secretary type up all my poems and bind them in a black three-ring notebook so that I could display my twisted little psyche to unwitting victims at a moment's notice.

As the years went by, I expanded my range to include sex, swear words, and shocking religious references. I also discovered the poetry reading, the perfect vehicle for my exhibitionistic tendencies. At my first reading ever, I had several friends with me onstage. They held up large charcoal drawings of tampons and spaceships. The performance dealt with my sordid one-night stands, my hopeless romances, and my period. People loved it.

Dizzy with success, I replied to a classified ad seeking topless dancers. Could exposure redeem my imperfect body the way it had my flawed personality? I arrived at my audition with nothing to wear but my cotton underwear and high-top sneakers, had to use Scotch Tape instead of pasties, and selected some unbelievably slow Rod Stewart song for my music. It was the longest six minutes of my life. Was my face red.

*   *   *

Even when one explains something as best one can, one can't be sure what the listener actually heard. It is terrible to think one's confessions have been misunderstood. One wakes up the next morning feeling marred, as if the person in the mirror were someone else. As if one were driving a personality with a broken windshield. As if there were something wrong with the light. These invigorating feelings are often combined with a hangover.

Yes, once again one has had too much to drink and could not be shut up all night long. One has lectured one's friends about their faults. Criticized the way they treat their girlfriends. Chided them for not confiding their troubles, while boring them to tears with one's own. Wound up the evening by sharing the exact price one paid for their birthday presents.

For days, the half-remembered conversation looms large in one's mind. Thinking, endlessly thinking, too much, too loud, too thoughtless, too silly, too dull. Plotting, endlessly plotting, to be reinstated. Calling, endlessly calling, to rehash the thing on the phone. Writing, endlessly writing, newspaper articles, radio broadcasts, books of personal essays.

Finally one starts to feel a little better.

I think I should tell about the grocery store. Sometimes when something seems a little overpriced, I consider just slipping it into my bag. Then I picture myself being driven away in a police car, my children standing on the curb with tears on their cheeks. Later, in a cell, one arm cuffed to the bed, I write a letter to Dear Abby with the stub of a pencil. Sometimes this works; sometimes I find a mysterious tin of anchovies in my purse.

I make long-distance personal calls at work. Run letters through the postage meter. At one job I took home a bookshelf and a bunch of folding chairs. No one noticed. Sometimes I don't wear my seat belt. Once, I made up a big lie about getting robbed in a taxicab and went on about it for days. I can't even remember why anymore.

A long time ago, a counselor at camp used to play a song her brother had written on the guitar. I learned all the words and the chords. For years afterward, I told people I had written that song.

I was waiting in line to order a tall half-caf-half-decaf low-fat latte at an espresso bar in Boulder, Colorado. The hip-looking businessman in front of me—white shirt, shoulder-length hair, wire-rimmed shades —ordered an oatmeal chocolate chip cookie with his coffee. The *barista* raised his eyebrows knowingly. Back for that again? he asked.

It's the best cookie in the world, the man told me as he turned to find a table. Don't have one. It's like a shot of cocaine in your arm. Once you do it, you can never stop. Never.

My eyes widened, in what probably appeared to be
innocent amazement though it was, on the contrary,
informed amazement. It is a comparison you would
never make unless you *knew*, and here he was, with his
James Tayloresque receding hairline, saying he knew.

Naturally I ordered one, but the caloric little Frisbee
was not the same for me as it was for him. For me, the
shot of cocaine is the act of revelation, be it mine or the
cookie man's, or that of the mild-mannered marketing
consultant who told me, as we sat waiting for the check
after an ordinary work-related round of cocktails, how
he managed to eliminate his main rival in winning the
heart of the woman to whom he is married.

After asking him personal questions for several minutes, I had wandered onto the subject of how he met his
wife. His detailed response surprised and pleased me,
but what I will never forget is what he described as "the
turning point." *Kristy Ann and I were in the bar where
she worked, and this guy who she used to date was sort
of hovering around us, insulting me and trying to get her
to leave with him. Very calmly, I just reached over and
put out my cigarette in his hand.*

Jesus, what a rush. I could hardly believe this guy
had ever smoked, much less that he had mutilated someone for love, or that he would tell me about it, with that
unmistakable mixture of pride and nonchalance and
irony and sheepishness and need. I looked back into his
eyes and gave him everything he wanted. Suddenly, we
were not alone.

This Is Not My Beautiful House

As I informed the Bureau of the Census in 1990, I continue to live my middle-income thirtysomething Caucasian life in a house of six rooms in Austin, Texas, with one Caucasian husband and two Caucasian sons and no unrelated persons who don't normally live here but don't have anyplace else to live either. Is this me? I thought as I filled in the last machine-readable block. A grown-up? A nuclear mom? A Donna Reed for the nineties?

I'll tell you, I didn't start out with this in mind. A born iconoclast, an aspiring artiste, a feminist vegetarian prodigal daughter, from early youth I considered myself destined to lead a startling life far outside the bounds of convention. I would be famous, dangerous, brilliant, and relentlessly cool: a sort of cross between Emma Goldman, Jack Kerouac, and Georgia O'Keeffe.

Home ownership, marriage, and gainful employment did not figure in my plans, except as symbols of the wimpy conformism I vowed to avoid. So what happened? Where did this station wagon come from? When did Ms. Emma O'Kerouac take up residence at the middle of the American road?

Escorted by the Ghost of Census Past, let us revisit the year 1980. Having graduated two years earlier from college—where I studied Hinduism, Marxism, and poetry to prepare me for what I supposed was my future—I drifted south to Austin. There I got a job teaching creative writing to juvenile delinquents, a position for which I was qualified by virtue of being hardly more than a creative delinquent myself. I lived in a house with the same number of rooms as my current home but half the rent and three times the number of inhabitants. Unrelated by blood or marriage, we were entwined instead by coincidence and convenience, by illicit love and left-wing politics, by the overarching need to agree on a single grocery list. I was twenty-three and suffering from delusions of grandeur, having just had my first book of poetry published in an edition of one thousand by a small press in New Braunfels, Texas! Convinced that fame and fortune awaited me, I packed up and moved to New York City.

Alas, I not only did not achieve instant celebrity but could not even find a place to live. At first, I stayed in the Alphabet City apartment of a family friend, a Buddhist on retreat with his lama. Later I moved in with a cordial but neurotic woman ten years older than I who charged me half the rent for the opportunity to put a bed in her walk-in closet. Dear Janice. She was the only remaining noninstitutionalized member of her wealthy Westchester family, but everything was fine between us until I ate her broccoli. Did I know she was planning to take this particular dish of leftover steamed broccoli to her poor crazy mother in the hospital? I'm telling you, this woman could have bought the entire 1981 broccoli crop of the United States and had money left over.

Getting out of there was no simple matter. By this time I was well aware that finding an apartment in New York is not simply a full-time job; it is an endeavor on a par with spinning straw into gold. Every Wednesday at six A.M. I bundled myself down to Sheridan Square to get the new edition of *The Village Voice*. Dozens of other mittened and scarved apartment seekers clustered around the boarded-up newsstand, waiting for the warm stacks of fresh papers to arrive. Greedy as pigeons, we grabbed up our copies and rushed off, praying to read faster and dial more speedily than our competitors.

From the moment I saw it in the paper, I had a feeling about LOWER CHELSEA WALKUP. Unabashed at the early hour, I dialed the number given in the ad. A recorded voice offered to take my message.

Oh, please, sir, rent me the apartment, I begged, continuing my supplications until there was a click and a sleepy voice came on the line.

Wazzamatta, you crazy? he asked.

With offers of bagels and coffee and six months' rent in cash, I bribed him to meet me at the apartment. My sister, Nancy, went with me; we ran the whole ten blocks, tossing a dollar to every bum we passed. At the door of the building, our future landlord awaited, grumpy and red-haired. He grudgingly accepted the deli bag and led us up four flights of steep linoleum-covered steps to the decrepit but definitely livable Apartment 16.

And we lived there, Nancy and I and her lover, Steven, and my old friend Sandye from New Jersey, in three tiny rooms in a commercial neighborhood, where an industrial exhaust fan blew dirty steam through the open windows and huge trucks thundered down the street every morning well before dawn. Those of us who liked the others to begin with fared all right, but those who didn't grew lush and verdant vines of hatred, sprouting around their ankles like ivy and rooting them to the spot.

One night a man who was visiting Sandye jumped up from the bed at three A.M. I've got to go, he said, stepping over my pallet on the kitchen floor. I can't sleep here. It's the trucks.

Or did he say "the drugs"? Either one made sense to us; we didn't get much sleep in that place ourselves. The landlord, it had turned out, was a junkie. We could tell that he'd been by to visit when we found our teaspoons bent and blackened behind the commode.

But the housing situation was not my worst problem.

Even more frustrating was the fact that the city of my birth was a veritable Marion Winik factory, a city overrun by Marion Winiks, all wearing the same cute outfits, writing the same short stories, taking the same trains to the same parties to talk about the same movies with the same people. Living in Texas, I had benefited from a certain émigré mystique; I so rarely met someone "just like me" that I was able to sustain an illusion of uniqueness.

In New York, it was another story. All this competition, this constant affront to my cherished individuality, made me feel exceedingly lethargic. What with this and the nearly simultaneous breaking of my heart by a guy I was absolutely sure was my soul mate, I turned to drugs. Actually, I had already turned to drugs, but now I embraced them with a vengeance. My life was already ruined anyway.

Midway through my brilliant demise, I was rescued by Destiny, or at least by Sandye, who crammed me into a blue Peugeot full of Manhattanites heading down to Mardi Gras in New Orleans. There I fell madly in love with a sexually ambiguous ice-skating bartender named Tony. Though I was not really his type, he couldn't resist my air of passionate excess: She carries a whole carton of cigarettes in her purse, he bragged to his friends. Enraptured, I sat at his bar every night till he got off at three A.M., when we'd dance and drink and do drugs in the men's room and walk the smelly oyster-juice streets until dawn.

My carnival beau had a wonderful apartment in the French Quarter, a second-floor studio with an iron-railed balcony and red brick walls. The kitchen window opened above the courtyard of a guest house for gay men, and bits of gossip and details of meals at Gallatoire's and Arnaud's drifted in all day long. How could I resist? Within a week after returning home, I broke the news to my roommates, quit my job, and made arrangements to finish my master's degree by mail. I knew the relationship was a little iffy, but I had to get out of New York somehow.

The first few months were rocky, complicated by his ex-lovers and my neuroses, but neither of us was ready to give up. Instead we decided to bid the French Quarter adieu. We would cement our coupledom by starting a new life in a new town, by tossing every last bean into the cooking pot. Soon we were dragging a U-Haul filled with our mutual possessions back to Austin, where low rents and ephemeral job offers beckoned.

We leased an unair-conditioned house on the Avenue of Confederate Heroes, where planes cruised overhead almost close enough to touch. But what was wrong with this place ran deeper than jet engines, deeper than nautical wallpaper and peeling linoleum. It was sheer exhaustion, the weariness of a rent house that has been filled and emptied too many times, that sprawls on its corner with a beaten look, slouch-framed door wide open.

At first, I thought the house was fine. I was right

back there in the sweaty kitchen cooking lentil soup on the crooked stove. But gradually, the funkiness of the place came to seem overwhelming, not inspiring. As my zest for antimaterialism began to fade, I lost interest in making do with less. I wanted new things, clean things, things that worked when you turned them on, things with five-year warranties on parts and labor. I wanted central air and heat. What you want, said the real estate agent, is a condominium!

It wasn't painless, leaving postadolescent bohemia behind, becoming a typical yuppie couple, acquiring the trendy condo to complete the picture. But suddenly the promise of gracious living—the luminous planes of unspoiled Formica—seemed to outweigh the once-dreaded bourgeois connotations. (Tony, on the other hand, he of the fabulous French Quarter, had no such radical pretensions to wrestle with. Ready for gracious living from the word go, he was delighted that I had finally come around.)

It's okay, I thought. I'm buying a house, not selling my soul. It's not as if I'd started wearing high heels and voting Republican. It's not as if I owned a microwave oven, for God's sake. I may have relaxed my standards, but I haven't lost them altogether.

I looked at one place after another, but most of them had a certain generic hotel-room feeling that failed to enchant. Finally the wily real estate agent took me to the construction site of a condominium that had not yet been built. As he suspected, this place had none of the flaws of those that already existed. I could tell from the tiny floor plan with its clever symbols, it was just perfect. The neighborhood was perfect. Even the trees that had to be cut down to make way for the complex were perfect. But what's this here? I asked, pointing to an unfamiliar symbol in the rectangle marked "Kitchen." A built-in microwave, the agent told me confidently. Oh well, I rationalized, I'll never use it.

Reversing the pattern followed by previous generations, home ownership led us somehow to marriage. I had always assumed I wouldn't marry. It was just too predictable, too passé. Though I did feel attracted to motherhood, I hoped to pull it off without accumulating a husband in the process. As it turned out, I accepted my first proposal. It came one night while Tony and I were lying on the bed after a gin game with my newly-wed sister, Nancy, and brother-in-law, Steven. Do you think we should get married too? asked my partner at cards, as we held hands, watching a silent television. Yes, I said slowly, I do.

I had finally figured it out—the way my life felt from the inside was more important than how it looked from without. And how I felt was neither predictable nor passé. And so I entered the state of holy matrimony—in ivory lace, no less, champagne in one hand, cigarette in the other. This is the happiest day of my life, I announced to my uncle behind the video camera. I was trying to sound facetious, but my starry eyes gave me away.

A couple of years passed. I quit smoking and had a baby; the trendy condo was transformed as well. My sunny study became a nursery, the elegant guest bath Diaper Central, our plush silver wall-to-wall carpet a grizzled mat. The flight of steps leading to our front door gradually assumed the aspect of Sisyphus's mountain; a toddler played the role of the rock. The last straw came one day as I was pushing him to the store for some juice. He pitched himself out of the stroller and bolted into someone else's backyard. A little slide, a toy car, and a plastic rake—he thought he was in Disney World. The owner drove up just as I was dragging him away. I'm sorry, I told her, he doesn't have a yard of his own.

I had the marriage, I had the kid, we had just bought the station wagon, now all I needed was the two-car garage to park it in. To be honest, by this time I didn't give a damn how conventional my dream house might be; I just wanted a place where we could spread out and be a family. So as the first months of the nineties unfurled, my little clan and I moved to a spacious abode with a big kitchen and a verdant expanse of fenced yard, which we immediately equipped with a plastic rake and a fleet of small engineless vehicles.

So that's how it happened. And I'm not the only one it's happened to, either. Most of the people we have barbecues with and watch *L.A. Law* with and borrow baby clothes from are erstwhile rebels and renegades, each of whom could write a Big Chill baby boomer bildungsroman of his or her own. Does it mean we don't care about art or politics or God or what is cool and what is not? I don't think so. It just means we fell in love and got too old to stay up all night and moved on, with a little more baggage, to the next hotel.

For Mr. Turtle, and Others

The flat goldfish floating at the top of the bowl, the stiff cat hanging from the chain-link fence, the weary dog driven, hot-nosed and trustful, to the vet for the very last time. The Easter bunny that drew blood from a childish thumb and disappeared, cage and all, the next day. The crazy fox terrier who did not want to be dressed up as King Henry the Eighth, who dive-bombed the sprinkler, who terrorized the slumber party, who went after Scott Sugarman bare-toothed and growling and was sucked by Mrs. Sugarman's righteous wrath into the back of a Pet Control truck. The gerbil Rock, mate of Roll, chased under the living-room couch by the cat, where safe at last, he keeled over from a heart attack. That same gerbil-loving tabby, emaciated after three months lost in the woods, suddenly mewing at the door just as we were leaving for vacation. Entrusted to a neighbor, she had to be buried in the garden while we were gone.

If childhood pets teach responsibility, they also teach the limits of love. To feed and to walk and to brush and to sift through the litter box, not just when you feel like it but every day, every day because THIS IS YOUR PET. YOU TAKE CARE OF HIM. DON'T YOU THINK I HAVE ENOUGH TO DO AROUND HERE? Pee on the paper, Buddy. On the paper, do you hear? No, don't eat those shoes. Don't chew on the electrical wire. GET OUT OF THE STREET, BUDDY! HURRY! HOW MANY TIMES DO WE HAVE TO TELL YOU? But ultimately all our affection and careful custodianship cannot keep Buddy alive, and only the meanest person would use the word "roadkill" to describe an animal killed in the road.

Dustin, Tiger, Missy, Brandy, Pumpkin, Buzz, Noodles! Shep, Schnapps, Zeke, River, Conga, Rufus, Ali Baba, Fluffy the Whore! The names echo through the neighborhood, the plaintive whistles from yard to yard, the photocopied signs stuck hopefully on phone poles. VERY FRIENDLY. WHITE WITH BLACK SPOTS. GENEROUS REWARD. Every day at dinnertime I ran the electric can opener by the open window, hoping the lost kitty would dream of a blue dish of moist tuna and come limping home. I would have liked to wear a silver bracelet like the ones we wore for soldiers missing in Vietnam—BUTTERBALL, and the date he disappeared, stamped in capital letters in the metal.

It is less complicated to love a pet than a person, but it takes more imagination to mourn one. How can a grown woman properly express her grief over the death of a cockatiel? I think back to Mr. Turtle, his head tucked in once and for all, laid to rest in a small box by child mourners in black witch gowns from last Halloween. The Irish wake for the Irish wolfhound, the Jewish social worker who sat shivah for a faithful Dane. Our friend Jeff, who buried his Lucia in the piney woods near a stream, a Doberman outfitted like Cleopatra with studded collar and fresh-picked flowers, favorite possessions and snacks for her journey to the afterlife. Poems by Wallace Stevens and Dylan Thomas copied out on slips of paper, read by Jeff and his girlfriend over the grave.

My friend Paul Basil lost his dog Lilly five years ago. Paul drew lines with people but never drew a line for that dog, a sleepy black Lab with a white star on her chest. She suffered his human sweethearts with patience, knowing their tenure in her waterbed was only temporary. Sure enough, each girl eventually left in despair. *God, Paul, I only wish I was that dog.* At the end, he nursed Lilly and cleaned up after her without minding and for months he was awkward with the sorrow of it, the back of his truck as empty as his heart.

Though he was always kind to strays, Paul never got another dog; he never really settled down with a woman either. He lavished a lot of care on automobiles and remote-control planes and carpentry projects, as if no living thing would ever belong to him again. Then one Saturday night he was driving home from a camping trip in New Mexico, and a drunk heading the other way crossed into his lane and hit Paul's car at a hundred miles per hour.

I see the accident over and over in my mind, and sometimes I see it like this: Just as the headlights blinded him, as the terrible crunching began, that tunnel of golden light you hear so much about opened up in the roof of the car. Floating out of the contracting front seat and the sudden shards of glass and metal, he soared straight up above the highway into the West Texas sky. And as he moved out of the tunnel through the luminous gateway, Lilly stood there waiting, her brown eyes wet, her nose lifted high, her whole stumpy body wagging with anticipation.

Sixteen Pictures of My Father

1. A small, square black-and-white photograph with a scalloped white edge on which the date May 1959 is printed in small type. I am the curly-headed baby in a white party dress sitting up on Daddy's shoulder eating a strawberry. Boyishly handsome in his crew-neck sweater and grown-out GI haircut, he smiles up at me, squinting into the sun. He is thirty, I am one, we are in love.

2. Twenty-five years later. My father and I at my sister's wedding, a beautiful summer day at the golf club. We are facing each other in profile, mouths wide open, very excited, talking at once. We are running the show. My father looks like Lee Iacocca with his white hair and his wire-rimmed glasses. The day he started wearing those glasses was the day he was no longer

young. If you look at this photograph long enough, my father disappears. I am alone in my fuchsia party dress, in profile, mouth wide open.

3. Nights when our parents are out, Nancy and I make Jiffy-Pop and show sixteen-millimeter home movies on the wall of the den. Our favorite is Mommy and Daddy on their honeymoon. They wear matching tennis sweaters and pretend to paddle around the empty swimming pool at Grossinger's. Young and happy, they hardly ever get on each other's nerves.

4. My father in flowered velvet bell-bottoms and a denim safari jacket, his wild gray hair sticking out all over the place. It is very late at night and he is at his discotheque, the Pandemonium, where Brother Duck is playing and everyone is drinking Harvey Wallbangers and smoking pot. The Pandemonium is losing money like crazy. My mother is home, loading the dishwasher and crying, mostly because he looks so ridiculous and he won't cut his hair. I hear her the next morning on the phone: He is a forty-three-year-old man, for Christ's sake.

5. In this picture, my father is writing a check. This check will feed me and clothe me and send me to college, will pay for my eyeglasses, my summer camp, my abortion, my psychiatrist, and my phone bill, will insure my car and fix my nose and take me out to dinner

on my birthday. Stereos, TV sets, diet pills, guitar lessons, collect calls from Europe, all covered. This is a very important check, but my father scribbles it out quickly, and hands it to me without looking up. Here you go, sport, he says.

6. This is a twenty-mile-long traffic jam created by New Jersey commuters trying to get into Manhattan. All eight zillion of them have to squeeze in by nine A.M. through two underwater tunnels or over a bridge. My father is not in this traffic jam—are you kidding? He gets off the turnpike, goes through the underpass, down the frontage road, over a bridge, zigzags through parking lots and shopping centers and the sleeping downtown streets of Union and Weehawken, gets back on the turnpike at a different exit only to cut off again and loop around, winding up ten minutes later at the front of the line. All the while he is listening to Chapter 6 of *War and Remembrance* on his cassette player and figuring out how to do a spreadsheet in Lotus 1-2-3 that will automatically compute the winnings for the Super Bowl pool.

7. My father is in his office at his perennially failing textile firm. He has an unusual group of employees, who have all been there forever and are devoted to him beyond reason. The tiny, ancient bookkeeper; the flamboyant male receptionist; the disheveled, disreputable delivery man; the enormous bald computer operator from

Long Island. At his desk, my father yells, Edna! Harold! Junior! Artie! Get in here! And his motley minions assemble to do his bidding.

8. We have the coolest father on the street. He plays war with all the kids on the hill behind the Mahoneys', takes us on Lost Rides in the car, teaches us about schneiders and double schneiders and other secrets of scoring for world-class gin rummy. We have a movie of him jumping rope, totally flat-footed, bringing his knees all the way up to his chin on every jump. He answers the front door in his boxer shorts. When I was very young, I thought he was Fred Flintstone.

9. Fred Flintstone is not amused when I call at two o'clock in the morning because the car has broken down on the way home from the rock concert, and six of us are stranded in a police station somewhere near Passaic, a good hour away from home. Morons! he says, stomping into the police station in his pajamas. Get in the goddamn car!

10. My father is having a heart attack in his Cadillac El Dorado during morning rush hour in the middle of the Lincoln Tunnel. He grimaces but continues driving into the city, where he parks his car in his customary spot on the roof of the Port Authority Bus Terminal and proceeds to his dentist appointment. You look like hell, Hyman, says the dentist. My father can barely reply.

The dentist calls an ambulance. My father's hospital-
ization coincides with the publication of *Iacocca!*, the
autobiography of his corporate Italian look-alike. He
receives about a dozen copies from various well-wishers.

11. Some years later, my father has a coronary bypass operation, after which he will eat nothing but
chicken salad. Not just any chicken salad, we soon
learn, as the nurses' refrigerator fills up with rejected
deli containers. It should have large chunks of white
meat! Maybe a little celery! Not this goddamn chicken
paste! Soon everyone who visits is bringing chicken
salad for his review. Now this is chicken salad, Hy. Try
this. We drive in from Jersey with chicken salad made
by his mother, the famous Gigi. Although this is certainly the salad against which all others must be mea-
sured, even it is not eaten with real gusto. They say my
father will recover, as 99 percent of bypass patients do,
but they are wrong.

12. I land at Newark Airport upon my return from
New Mexico, where I have spent two weeks in the mountains with my guru. I am seventeen years old, barefoot,
and wrapped in a Navajo blanket. Where the hell are
your shoes, he says. Get in the goddamn car!

13. My father's body is lying in a box at the
Bloomfield-Cooper Funeral Home, where my mother,
sister, and I go to see it before it is cremated. I have

never seen my father dead and I have never seen him
wearing a yarmulke either, so this is a double surprise.
I fear that this awful picture will stay with me forever
and blot out all the other pictures of him in my mind,
but later I can remember only that his head seemed too
large for his body, the yarmulke, and his closed eyelids.

14. The last time I saw my father alive and well was
the ignominious night he bailed us out of jail in New York
City. My sister, Nancy, her husband, Steven, my then-
fiancé, Tony, and I (Dey got yuh whole family? a fellow
prisoner inquired incredulously) squirmed on the
wooden bench, sobered up and scared to death after
twenty-four hours in Manhattan's central holding tank.
Too impatient to drive back to the apartment after scoring, we'd pulled over on a darkened street with our little
packets of powder; the car was surrounded by cops in less
than a minute. Out in the courtroom, my father was white
with exhaustion and anger. It was after midnight when
the judge set our fines and let us go. We were ashamed
and miserable, but Daddy took us out to a restaurant,
where we ate and drank by candlelight and soon were
reminiscing about jail as if it were years instead of hours
in the past. At four A.M., he left for home. We watched
him drive off through a dense white fog.

15. Before you lose a parent, you think, Oh God,
what will I do if one of them dies? Then it happens, and
you find out you can't do anything. You just go on.

Maybe you can try to become what you miss most. My
father is not in this picture, but his shoulders are. I wear
the memory of those football-player shoulders like a
magic cloak, indispensable for getting through traffic
jams.

16. This is the face I remember best. He's in a swimming pool on one of those floating lawn chairs, drinking
a Heineken. The two dogs jump in and paddle over to
throw themselves into his lap, the gangly Lab pup and
the miniature dachsund. The shutter snaps as he begins
to topple in, surprised, laughing, holding the beer aloft.

Women Who Love Men Who Don't Pay Their Parking Tickets

He's the type of guy you can't resist: an eccentric jazz musician, a pothead, a hothead, a drinker, a dreamer, a drifter, an existential philosopher with great dimples and amazing hands. His eyes are the color of the ocean outside the cottage where you spent summers as a child. Some days he reminds you of Charles Manson. Others, he is as gentle and helpful as Flipper.

Soon you are spending all your free time in jazz clubs. I thought you hated jazz. Well, not anymore. Next thing, you move into his little garage apartment. It's so bohemian. So masculine. We're talking federal disaster area.

At first you don't notice that he never has any money. Then you do notice. You especially notice one sweet spring day when he phones from the police station, and you pay hundreds of dollars in overdue fines, as well as a hefty fee to an unsympathetic attorney, to redeem your newfound beau from the clutches of the state.

Son, says the judge, don't let me catch you behind the wheel of a car in this county again.

Those assholes, he rages as you leave the courtroom. I wouldn't want to drive a golf cart in this backwater dump.

He gets mad; she gets a receipt.

Have you ever thought that if you could only have seen the turning point, the moment when things started to go wrong, you would have ended it right there and prevented all the pain and confusion and emotional slamdancing that came afterward? Well, this is it.

But you can't do it. He needs you. You need him. You love each other. And don't the breathless highs make the dreadful lows worthwhile? Isn't it better than dating the nephew of your mother's bridge partner? Okay, okay, so stay with him. Spend the rest of your life at the Blue Note. Breaking up is like having a tooth pulled: you don't just do it the minute you get a toothache. You wait until your existence is a living hell, alternative treatment is no longer possible, and getting it yanked seems less painful and scary than keeping it in your mouth another day.

Does this scenario sound familiar? If so, you may be one of us: Women Who Love Men Who Don't Pay Their

Parking Tickets. To see whether you are at risk, take this simple test. Who is sexier: Paul McCartney or Jim Morrison? Ron Howard or James Dean? George Bush or Che Guevara? Subtract your boyfriend's IQ from his bank balance. If you get a negative number, give yourself two points. Which of the following couples best exemplifies your romantic ideal: Bonnie and Clyde. Gregg Allman and Cher. Simone de Beauvoir and Jean-Paul Sartre.

There are no right and wrong answers, only right and wrong people. For you, only Mr. Wrong will do. You seek him out with deadly accuracy, as if your X-ray eyes could bore through the back pocket of a faded pair of Levi's, into the tattered wallet, through the folded scraps of paper and guitar picks and parking tickets. Ah ha! Two dollars and thirty cents! You home in like a Japanese beetle to the gardener's sex lure.

The roots of this fatal attraction may lie in the psychoeconomic circumstances of your childhood. To a young girl growing up in a typical middle-class suburban family, whose members spend more time relating to their appliances than to one another, poverty may seem irresistibly romantic. After all, compare your own household with the poor but close-knit March family of *Little Women*: Meg, Jo, Beth, Amy, Marmee. The more deprivation they suffer, the more wonderful they become! At your house, everyone is selfish and bored out of their mind.

But you are different, you are special, and you are

going to get the hell out of there. The easiest way to rebel is to date an established rebel. Without a cause, without a credit card, without the keys to the family car, rebels are sexy in ways that acceptable young men are not. And there they are, right out in the high school parking lot.

God, it's great. The wind blowing through your hair, the leather jacket against your skin, the taste of straight tequila in your mouth. His friends, their crooked smiles, enormous tattoos, and exhilarating prison records. You want to dress like them, talk like them, smoke like them. Steal them steaks from your parents' freezer. Like Patty Hearst, you want to change your name to Tanya.

You grow up, but your taste in men does not. You still go for outlaws: radicals, artists, writers, street people, any kind of perennially unemployed nonconformist. However, a new dynamic has developed. Just a few months into the relationship, you begin to be annoyed by exactly those qualities that attracted you in the first place. You find yourself trying to reform your angry young man, trying to make him get a job, open a checking account, quit doing so much coke, come home at a decent hour, make his bed.

Here you were going to be a biker chick and you've turned into Felix Unger. Or a disturbingly accurate imitation of your own mother. You are now in the painful second stage of this affliction, where the urge to rebel gives way to the urge to rehabilitate. You still think you want a moody maverick with fire in his eyes, but what you really want is a guy who will bring over some wine and a video and snuggle up beside you on the couch. Then you find one, and he bores you to tears.

You decide to take a vacation with one of your girl-friends, just forget about men for a while. They can all go to hell, you proclaim, toasting your resolve with air-plane cocktails. Then, the first morning on the beach, you meet a blond surfer from Prague with a great body and a degree in political science. A gorgeous penniless Marxist beach bum. Perfect.

After five dreamy days and enchanted evenings on the beach and in the thatch-roofed hut, you know this is more than just a vacation romance. You invite him to come back to the States and stay with you for a while.

He is fun to walk down the street with, fun to talk to, fun to sleep with. Everything is great. Well, sort of great, anyway. You begin to tire of his inexhaustible and vocal disdain for American culture. The political provincialism, the television shows, the cuisine. He knows all about it because while you're at work every day, he's back at your comfortable air-conditioned apartment, reading the paper, watching TV and eating takeout.

Haven't you read this script enough times to know that this guy doesn't have your missing glass slipper? Every self-help book in the bookstore, every codepen-dent in your support group, every planet in your chart says he's got to go. But his eyes are the color of the Caribbean lapping the sand of Isla Mujeres; as always, he needs you you need him you love each other.

The irresistible slamdancing toothache takes you in his golden anti-imperialist arms, and you *are* Tanya: purse full of steaks, riding into the Harley sunset.

How Do I Look?

never dreamed I would be the mother of boys. It seemed physically impossible that my body could manufacture one. Having grown up in a house where everyone was female except my father, I never knew much about my peers of the opposite sex. They were as Other as you can get; I understood them only in terms of their effect on me. They frustrated me, fascinated me, bored me, eventually drove me crazy with desire. I set up paper dolls of them in my head and they ran my life.

Yet it is probably for the best that I'm raising sons. Though they're still too small to be certain, I think I can stand to let them become who they are without interfering too much. The few things I know about what makes a decent man in this world I'm not afraid to pass on. If I had a daughter, I would be terrified of stuffing her full of all the sick shit I grew up with, of poking and prying and picking and not letting go. Yes, I've arrived at Womanhood but don't ask me for directions. The path I took was dark and circuitous and I fell down all the time and got broken. Even now I'm not sure I'm out of the woods. How could I let my little girl try to find her own way? How could I help but take her to the very same places I've been?

Sometimes I think childhood memories are fabricated like pearls around a grain of sand. You know how it works: take one old photograph and the quick current of memory it sparks; add what you heard happened, what could have happened, what probably happened; then tell the story over and over until you get the details down. It doesn't take a degree in psychology to reverse-engineer your childhood based on the adult it produced.

Even if I've made it all up, it doesn't matter. I'm stuck with the past I believe in, even if it's wrong.

It was a long time ago. I was a tiny girl, no, I was never a tiny girl, I was a blobby girl, or, as I often thought to myself, just a blob. I was not like the girls in the stories, at least not in the stories I liked. I was all wrong, I was not right, I was ashamed. Did I say a long time ago, I meant last week.

Something was wrong with me. Intellectually I was a wonder but physically I was a catastrophe. My parents tried to help. Nothing escaped their solicitous and well-meaning attention, not my feet, my eyes, my nose, my teeth, my weight (which was every part of me, when you think of it), not even the slight lisp I had in early grade school.

A podiatrist equipped me with various orthopedic devices to correct the minor imperfections of my lower extremities. I had a belt with attached rubber hoses that went down both legs to plates on the soles of my shoes. I don't remember ever wearing it, only seeing it in the attic years later and shuddering to think. When I started school, I pitched a big enough fit to have this monstrosity exchanged for a pair of oxblood clodhoppers with white-green hard plastic inserts. I had to wear the right shoe on the left foot and the left shoe on the right foot as if I didn't know any better. This did not go unnoticed by the vicious brats on the playground.

I had a good story, though, for anyone who would listen. See, my father had taught me to stand on his hand and walk up his arm when I was not even nine months old and my baby bones were too soft and they curved from the pressure. This explanation fit in with my understanding that my mental superpowers, my precocity, were somehow tied to my physical spazziness. I was a freak of nature. The fact that I was a prodigy had warped me, misshaped me, made me ugly and uncoordinated. I had to pay.

I had a lazy eye, mysterious allergies, and crooked teeth, treated at length and in depth by appropriate specialists. I had surgery, I had shots every week, I did eye exercises where I focused on a pen light rigged up inside a cereal box while walking the length of the living room holding a pencil in front of my nose. My mother drove me to the city every few months to what I thought was called the Ioneer Clinic and only years later realized was the Eye and Ear. Tuesday mornings I was taken out of class to visit the speech therapist's office in the basement of the school. It was a dungeonlike room with bad lighting where we played imbecile card games that involved pronouncing words with the letter *S*. Snake. Scissors. Sorry.

My orthodontist, a perverse torturer who never liked me and had grotesque quantities of hair poking out of his nostrils, tightened my braces every month for four years. Toward the end, our relationship was so hostile that I snarled at him from the reclining chair like the little girl in *The Exorcist*. He finally ripped the braces off my teeth and threw me out. Even the hope of soaking my parents for another thou wasn't worth the trouble.

Haircuts too had a grim aspect. My mother took Nancy and me to her salon, with its stinky solutions, blasting hairdryers, and crowds of kvetching ladies getting their nails done. The despotic queen of this palace of poufery was a coiffeuse named Brigit, who terrorized me with her flawless Aryan glamour and the steely precision with which she trimmed our too-short bangs across our foreheads and applied her curling iron to our party hairdos.

Once every few months my mother would lighten my sister's dark blond hair with Midnight Sun, but mine was hopelessly brown.

All my other shortcomings paled beside my tendency to chubbiness, my most serious and intractable flaw. It seems now as if I were born on a diet, as if I drank skim milk instead of formula, as if the first book I ever read was a calorie counter. I was brought up to think of Ring Dings and HoHos and Yodels as pleasures beyond all conception, though whenever I got my hands on sweets I would eat them so fast I could barely taste anything. My sister was skinny; she got French fries and milk-shakes all the time. I finished them for her.

Would anyone like dessert? the waitress asked, and the look my mother shot me could have iced coffee.

By the time I reached preadolescence, I had embarked on an extended tour of the weight-loss regimes popular in the seventies, including Weight Watchers, Stillman, Atkins, Scarsdale, later the Beverly Hills, the Nashville Rotation, finally the Doctor's Eat Anything. Certain foods veered crazily between okay and not okay, like pistachio nuts, which you could binge on or not touch at all depending on whom you followed, and grapefruits, which you either consumed before every meal or shunned as absolutely inimical. You peeled the skin off the chicken, ate the hamburger without the roll, consumed nothing you didn't first weigh, count, or mea-sure. Eight glasses of water a day, a whole watermelon, gluey baked concoctions made from cottage cheese and egg yolks and Sweet'n Low. When cyclamates went off the market, my mother bought a carton of Sweet'n Low so gigantic that she has it still.

She took me to a diet doctor who gave me boxes full of red and yellow and blue pills, of which I was to take a dozen a day. I raced through school with a dry mouth, a pounding heart, and a personality that was hyper and brittle enough without prescription amphetamines, thank you. They didn't work for losing weight, so I tried to get boys to like me by giving them away. They didn't work for that either. The sturdy little boxes they came in, however, were good for burying dead goldfish and turtles.

A few years ago, I found a drawerful of letters my parents had written me while I was away at summer camp. I was touched by the frequency of their communication, the details of their golf games, news of my now-dead grandmother and cousins. But in every letter, every single letter, they asked if I was remembering to take my pills. Even Daddy did it, in the few that were written in his hand. As if the damn pills were vital to my continued existence. How was it that they believed that?

I saved my babysitting money to send away for the sauna pants advertised in the back of *Seventeen* magazine. They were mustard yellow knicker-length inflatable plastic horrors with a small hand pump attached. You put them on, blew them up, and did the exercises in the booklet (if you had over fifteen pounds to lose) or just lay around and watched TV (lucky you, less than fifteen to go). The idea was that you would sweat twice as much.

When the sauna pants proved ineffective, I fantasized about an authentic miracle implement, a magic scissors that would allow me to neatly trim off unwanted flesh without no muss, no fuss, no blood. I could look at my thighs and see exactly where to cut.

I developed the sick habit of looking at other girls and evaluating whether I'd like to have certain of their body parts. I wanted this one's incredibly white eye-whites, that one's vivacious little butt. Getting changed into our horrendous blue gymsuits, I'd spy around the locker room and select components of a new anatomy as if they were Colorforms. Her legs. No, maybe they're too skinny. Hers are better. Look at the ankles. No Neanderthal guy ever objectified women's bodies like this. I still do it sometimes. I can't help it.

I had read enough teen magazines and sent away for enough movie-star beauty booklets to know that I might be able to improve my desperate life overnight if I could only get the right hairdo. But the world of preteen hairstyles was a rigid one. At the time, the sole passport to popularity was parallel hair, an utter straightness achieved by setting it nightly on empty frozen-orange-juice cans. This technique was grudgingly demonstrated to me by a Girl Scout car-pool mate, a future cheerleader with freckles and a flip. I felt honored that she would even talk to me, let alone take me into her pink-and-white bedroom and show me her secrets. Her mother must have made her do it. Unfortunately, hair-rolling required way more small-muscle coordination than I had in my wildest dreams. And my family did not drink frozen orange juice.

In any case, I had given up on ever looking decent, much less beautiful or thin. I think it was in about fifth grade that I started purposely neglecting my appearance. Since I refused to go shopping at the store for fat people where my mother tried to take me, she had our cleaning lady, Dory, make me a blue tent dress with multicolored flower-power daisies and a floppy white collar. I wore it for days on end. My teacher came into the bathroom and tried to help me, pulling up my socks and brushing my hair and saying things would be better for me if I would change my dress. If I would just try a little. I hated her for doing this and knew that trying would get me nowhere.

Two years later, I tried to kill myself by taking a bottle of Bayer aspirin. I had gotten a C minus in English, and Michael Feinberg liked my friend, Sandye, better than me. I wrote a melodramatic poem, then lay down on my mother's bed. My mother came home just afterward and found me there. She didn't have to try too hard to get me to tell her what I had done. She snatched me up and dragged me to the car. Sixty seconds to your headache, she muttered, quoting the television commercial as we sped to the hospital. My stomach was pumped in the emergency room. Afterward I was sent to a psychiatrist. I convinced the shrink to tell my parents to cut out a few of my other doctors.

For my fourteenth birthday, my parents offered me a nose job. I refused.

One day in the car my mother told me that overweight girls sometimes make the mistake of sleeping with boys too easily because they think it will make them popular. Yeah, Ma, and if that doesn't work we just give them our diet pills.

But as thoughtless as her comment was, it was not completely off base. Ever since I got Glenn Willis to French-kiss me on the golf course, I had been chalking up sexual experiences as evidence of my physical okayness. As if they would add up to pretty. Of course it didn't work, because if you do it and they don't love you and don't want you anymore, that's evidence of your awfulness for sure.

Sometimes one of them would say I had beautiful eyes or nice shoulder blades and there would be nothing in the world like that joy. Like when my father used to admire my pinkies. Isn't it funny how I still believe there's something wonderful about my pinkies. I wonder if he could have done that for the rest of me as well.

Even now, there's a certain kind of teenage girl I can hardly stand to look at. She has lots of curvy flesh and

too-tight torn-up clothes and she thinks she wants to get
fucked but that is not it, that is not it at all. It is,
however, just what she will get.

By the time I went to college, I was a slob and proud
of it. I never wore makeup or dieted or jogged or went
shopping for clothes, and I wouldn't let any of that
Barbie doll brainwashing ever touch me again. I took
seminars with titles like "Ten Thousand Years of Slav-
ery: Women and Hair" and wrote papers about the semi-
otics of eye shadow and images of submission and
violence in magazine advertising. My own hair was a
messy brown thicket, which I cultivated and trimmed
myself with nail scissors, varying the length of my bangs
in accordance with my mood. Short was French revolu-
tionnaire at the barricades; long was sultry enigma.

I thought I was free.

Then I started mysteriously throwing up after every
meal. It was the weirdest thing. When I was a block
away from the dining hall, not feeling nauseated or anything, the meal I'd just eaten would reappear in my
mouth. When it first started, I wasn't even embarrassed
to run to the bushes or spit it out in a handy cup. I
thought I had some kind of gastrointestinal problem. I
went in for tests at the student health center, and they
said, No, there's nothing physical; it's all in your head.
This was before anybody knew the word "bulimia."

I was shocked and furious that they would even suggest such a thing. I was over all that, I was sure.

Even after I realized they were right, I couldn't stop. I'd keep eating and eating until I felt sick, then go to the bathroom and quietly puke. I came back to the table smiling, and ate some more. I never lost a pound from doing this, I might add.

During this period, my mother was in New Jersey, embarking on a business venture. She opened a figure salon called Inches Aweigh. It featured machines that would shake the fat off you; you didn't have to do a thing. These salons were supposed to have been a big success in Florida, but they didn't catch on in New Jersey. Personally, I never set foot in the place.

It's ironic, or perhaps predictable, that I married a hairdresser. Somehow, being in love with the person who did my hair loosened my psychological and political shackles. I sat enthralled in the purple Naugahyde chair as he moved around me in a slow circle, sliding the curving clips off his watchband and into a shifting pile of hair at my crown, nimbly switching between the blue comb and the silver scissors. We had plans for my hair, my love and I.

I'd begun to come round in my attitude toward my appearance, realizing that the infernal teen magazines were actually right. Liking the way you look really is the secret of outer beauty and inner peace. Still, I wasn't ready for the hard stuff, like diets, exercise, or shopping. Hair, it seemed, was a quicker fix, more pleasant, easier to control.

Beginning with Tony's matriculation at the Modern College of Cosmetic Science and continuing well into his salon years, I appeared with one style after another, each a little shorter than its predecessor, until finally the nape of my neck made its stunning debut on the social scene. Suddenly I was chatting knowledgeably about bobs and layers; I amazed my friends with my command of terms like "double weight line" and "forward graduation." I realized I could make my hair represent my entire fun fun fun personality, and started on colors, blond highlights, which we dyed blue, then purple. I had permanents and body waves and artificial dreadlocks.

Hanging around the salon, I finally caught on. Nobody talks about hair when they talk about hair. They don't tell the stylist, "Take an inch off the bottom" or "Layer the sides." No, the cut they have now is boring, old, bedraggled, a stupid-looking wimpy drag. What they want is something cool, carefree, modern. The stylist's back bars are littered with the pictures they bring in, the ones they've cut out and saved and carried around in their purses for weeks: movie stars, models, Demi Moore or Melanie Griffith, or that perennial Virginia Slims ad—Rapunzel in a business suit, tangled waves wildly mussed by off-camera fans. It's not so different from my old Colorforms game.

I live in a house full of guys, and I don't hate my body so much anymore. I don't know if it's the hairdo or the hairdresser himself, the babies I made and birthed and nursed, the weight I finally lost, the long bike rides I learned to love, the cute clothes I bought at the Gap, or the week at the spa. I had the damn nose job after all—after the nose was redesigned by an encounter with a hockey puck during my brief, undistinguished career as the only woman in an otherwise all-male ice hockey league. I even have makeup now. A week before my wedding, I rushed out to a department store to buy one of each from the nice lady at the cosmetics counter. "Lavender on the lid, violet in the crease," I repeated like a mantra.

More than any of that, or behind it, is the fact that I just grew up and got used to myself.

My little boys think I am the most beautiful woman in the world. They love to touch me, to cuddle with me, to see me dress up in party clothes and lipstick. Wear the sparkly dress, Mama, you look so pretty in it. Their infatuation rubs off on me, and I think other people catch it too.

How do I look? I look fine. I know it, because I keep checking to make sure, sucking in the flesh under my cheekbones, standing at a certain perfect angle when I face my reflection. There's still some pain in there, some desperation, I can't even touch.

You can figure out how to act, what to wear, how to fit in, how to get by, but you can't change what has hurt you most deeply, the thing you are always trying to heal. Even laughing about it doesn't make it go away. I don't know if I believe in recovery, not even the twelve-step kind. If you admit you are powerless over the thing that has hurt you, do you finally stop coming back for more?

Even if the woman I am now looks all right, the girl I was then never will. Her time is up. She is stuck in there, staring at herself in the mirror, wanting and wanting.

Suburban Teens on Acid,
1972–1975

When word got out that our high school had been deemed to have "the third worst drug problem in New Jersey," we were proud. Proud that our lily-white chunk of suburbia was right up there with tough cities like Newark and Trenton, who regularly whipped our butts in basketball and track. We had missed Woodstock, Haight-Ashbury, the Summer of Love, the idealism and innocence of the psychedelic pioneers. For us, the imitators, the second generation, The Trip went no farther than our parents' carpeted living rooms or the parking lot of the local shopping center. Religious experiences were limited to those that could be achieved by watching *Monty Python's Flying Circus* on the public television station, or playing a single David Bowie record over and over until morning.

The closest we got to the proverbial garden was a

sports arena in North Jersey, where we attended outdoor concerts, where Carolyn Mahoney and I spent my fifteenth birthday at a Grateful Dead concert. We arrived at two P.M. for a show that wouldn't start until dark, spread out our blankets as close to the stage as possible, bought a couple of hits of acid from a wandering vendor—*Purple microdot, blotter, windowpane! Strawberry fields, orange barrel, orange sunshine! Get your chemicals here, get your thai sticks, get your organic mescaline!*—and giggled and smoked cigarettes and talked to strangers all afternoon, so high that a simple trip to the bathroom was a quest of epic proportions.

Finally it got dark and the Dead came out and played, which was orgasmic and thrilling and endless. Everyone mouthed the words and played air guitar. When we were passed a pair of binoculars from a neighboring blanket, we squinted anxiously at Bob Weir (so cute), Jerry Garcia (the avatar), Phil Lesh, Mickey Hart, Keith and Donna Godchaux (Is she the one "Sugar Magnolia" was written about? Or "Scarlet Begonias"? We had analyzed the song lyrics as if they were the Talmud. We wanted to know everything). Tiny panes of brilliant color swirled through air; moving objects left dense trails behind them, as if they had been photographed with a very long exposure. Carolyn, I'm peaking, are you? It was already the best Dead concert I had ever seen, and I had been to eleven of them. Then they played my song, "Eyes of the World." Oh my God. Oh my God. I almost fainted. It was a half-hour version of a three-minute song and right in the middle of it, I swear, Jerry Garcia said Happy birthday. Carolyn heard it too.

Somehow we ended up with no ride home, so after the show we went out to the parking lot and started asking people which way they were headed. We got a ride from some guys from Yonkers who went two hours out of their way to take us down to Asbury Park. Carolyn puked out the window and it got plastered all along the side of their car. Then we both decided we had forgotten what we looked like and begged them to pull over somewhere so we could go in a ladies' room and look in the mirror. They actually did it. When we got home, they asked us for some water to get the puke off the car. It hosed off easily. Then they drove away.

We usually got acid from Laurie Leonardo, a burly girl who drove to New York City in her big white station wagon and bought Baggies full of it in Central Park. Her father was a cop. We thought she was the coolest thing on earth. After all the little tablets were sold, she would let us lick out the orange or purple powder in the bottom of the bag.

Indeed, the majority of the drug dealers in our area seemed to be the offspring of public servants. One Thanksgiving morning, Nancy and I arrived home after being out all night tripping at the house of the mayor of a neighboring town, whose son had a nice little business selling acid and angel dust. When we got home, my

mother was sitting at the table having coffee. For some
reason, she took our all-night absence quite calmly, and
we sat around filling her in on details of the decor at the
mayoral residence. Then I, who could not bear to spare
my parents from a single sordid detail of our teenage
lives, announced that we were tripping. What? asked
my mother. LSD, Mom, we took LSD and now we're
tripping. But see, everything's fine! We don't think we're
Jesus Christ.

I just wanted her to understand that it was okay, that
drugs were great, that all those horror stories she was
hearing were a bunch of propaganda. Yes, I wanted to
be a wild teenage rebel, but I wanted to do it with my
parents' blessing.

My mother sighed and got up to pour herself a second cup of coffee. Go on, you two, she said. Try to get
some sleep before your grandmother gets here.

My parents went on a trip to the Bahamas and left us
with Dory, a short Trinidadian woman with a seriously
ample bosom who had been our live-in housekeeper and
babysitter when we were little. One of my earliest memories is of standing on the counter to reach the Cocoa
Puffs box, which was stashed in a cabinet high up above
the stove. Dory came marching in and caught me in the
act. Get down from there, Mahrion Weeneek, she ordered in her island brogue. No, I said. You're not my
mother.

I am a beeg wooman and you are a little girl, Dory replied. Now get down.

My sister and I collapsed in hysterics. For months the funniest joke on earth was to stick out your chest as far as you could, point to your tits, and say, I am a beeg wooman and you are a little girl! Get it? A beeg wooman!

In honor of our parents' being out of town, we had a tripping party. A dozen of our friends came over and we all ate some blotter and went nuts. We tore up some sheets and tied ourselves together in a line, then paraded through the house with the lights off, chanting. Up in the attic we sat in a circle around a single candle and played an obscure game whose object was to blow out the flame and whisper "Suck my dick" before anybody else could.

This wildness went on until two in the morning, when disaster struck. From my parents' room, wherein Dory had been shut up all night, presumably sleeping, came the sound of a television turned to its maximum volume. We all panicked and tried to be very quiet, but the blaring continued. Everyone said I should go down and talk to Dory, but she wouldn't answer my knock.

Finally she came out and announced she had called her husband, Kelvin, who worked the night shift at the local hospital, and she was taking us all over to the emergency room right away. Doom! The party broke up immediately, we got in big trouble with our parents, and Dory hated our guts after that. She had her revenge years later when my mother hired her to sew my sister's wedding dress and she made the armholes a half size too small.

I was tripping with my boyfriend Jon Melnick at an Allman Brothers concert when I realized for the first time in a blinding flash that nonmenthol cigarettes were much better than menthol. I switched to non-menthol right then and there.

Another time I was lying in my bed at four in the morning, putting my thoughts down on lined notebook paper as fast as I could. It was amazing. I was seeing myself and my relationships from the outside for the first time. All the injustices and traumas of my adolescence were finally making some kind of sense—the convoluted ultraintense teenage world of undying love and passionate friendship and soul-searing rejections and blow jobs and drugs and abortions and high school and God knows what other agonies. I saw that everything in the world was part of nature, nature was part of the universe, and everything in the universe formed a pattern that was sensible and beautiful if you could only see it from a distance. Like the seasons, the food chain, the solar system, like the beautiful colored patterns I was seeing in the air even as I wrote. Perhaps I was seeing the molecular structure of air itself! Then the point of the pencil somehow chipped down the middle, so that each stroke made two thin parallel lines, and I just had to stop because everything was everything and it was too intense.

The Madonna About Town

A woman nursing her baby in a restaurant, on a park bench, at the hair salon, on a city bus, in a doctor's waiting room, in front of a terminal, at the mall. Even the enlightened few who think this is perfectly fine and natural may still feel a soupçon of discomfort when actually confronted with the breast-feeding pair. I remember what it was like, trying not to see the flash of pale flesh between the scrunched-up shirt and the baby head. It seemed a little out of place in a public venue, not quite like picking your nose, not quite like trying to extract your bikini underwear from between your cheeks, not quite like sticking your hand down the front of your boyfriend's blue jeans, but still, not totally appropriate. I remember thinking, This lady probably went to Woodstock.

Now I know the other side of the story. Picture yourself, a brand-new mother, going out to eat for the first time after the birth. You know you're going to have to nurse, and you're a little nervous. Your mother and grandmother have already called to put in their two cents: Please, darling, try to be discreet. Take a little blanket to throw over your shoulder.

At the restaurant, your worst fears are realized. There you are with your tiny whimpering bundle, miniature pink mouth stretched wide, head swiveling back and forth, searching, snorting, frantically rooting, while the giant breast with its mammoth nipple comes bobbing out of its restraints like the runaway boob in Woody Allen's *Everything You Ever Wanted to Know About Sex*, leaking milk down your rib cage, into your lap, everywhere but into the baby's mouth. The blanket which you modestly draped over your shoulder is swept aside by flailing infant arms, and with it goes all hope of discretion. Your garments are in disarray, your bosom half-exposed, your back is killing you, and your husband looks as if he's going to faint. But the little one has finally found the nipple and is earnestly sucking his way to nirvana. Are you going to risk disturbing him just to rearrange your limbs and clothing? Just then, the waitress brings your fettuccine. You watch it cool with longing.

By the time you finally master public breast-feeding, it's too late. Your baby is now too old to be nursed, in the opinion of 99.9 percent of the U.S. population, and they have no qualms whatsoever about telling you so. In fact, as soon as the baby is born, people want to know how long you're going to nurse. Oh, I guess I'll stop before he goes to college, you reply. At first, this answer gets polite laughter. Once the baby starts walking, they stop laughing. You are some kind of sick ticket. And God knows what you are doing to that child.

As one who has spent many drowsy predawn or late-afternoon hours in lala-land with her babe, curled up close together in bed, stroking his soft hair and skin, memorizing every feature of his face, as he contentedly and sweetly sucks at my breast, I am the first to admit that nursing is a sensual experience. Sometimes he opens his eyes and gazes up soulfully into mine. Sometimes he smiles in midsuck without missing a beat. Sometimes he caresses and tickles me with his tiny hand, or grabs a handful of flesh and kneads it rhythmically. I'm in love with the little guy, head over heels, what can I do. He can get my bra off faster than anyone I ever met, no hands at all, just a hungry look.

I remember I wasn't sure I was going to like it. It's pretty hard to imagine what nursing will be like when the only lips that have been pressed to your breast previously have been there for an entirely different reason. But then my son was born, and a few minutes later someone lifted him into the vicinity of my nipple. Ahh. He knew exactly what to do. And after a little nervousness about how to hold him, where to put him, and how to keep from suffocating him with a boob that was twice the size of his head, so did I.

I'm not the only one who has these feelings about

nursing. My friend Carole called up to ask me do I think it's worse in the eyes of society to enjoy nursing if you've got a boy or a girl. She's got a girl. Is she a secret lesbian? Is she turning young Emily Rose into a future lesbian? One time she nursed my son while he was spending the afternoon at her house, and she couldn't help thinking how much he looked like me. That's it. Lesbian for sure.

Another friend pointed out to me that when the baby nurses just long enough so that your milk lets down (a powerful, almost painful tingle in your breasts, nipples popping up with an audible *boing*, milk flowing steadily, hot and fast), and at that very moment the baby decides no, she doesn't want to nurse right now, and leaves you sitting there, tingling and dripping all by your lonesome, that must be just the way a guy feels when he gets a hard-on during a heavy petting session and then the girl says, Stop it, don't do that.

We've even speculated that the mother's breastfeeding style determines the child's later sexual proclivities. Do you talk to him while you do it? Or do you talk on the phone? Do you cuddle and caress, or are you strictly business? Do you do it in the backseat of the car? What about the laundromat? Or the ladies' room? Are you willing to try different positions?

I was visiting my old friend Carolyn Mahoney in Florida when my son was five weeks old, and we were sitting out by her pool with our babies. Hayes got that sad look on his face that a five-week-old gets when he experiences hunger and doesn't know what it is or how to make it stop. He began to utter small, pathetic sounds. What's a mother to do? Not having mastered discretion or even rudimentary modesty, I whipped off the top of my bathing suit and fed my baby. Carolyn's husband's jaw dropped. He said, Hey, forget the titty bar. I think I'll just stay here at La Leche League.

The problem, of course, is the breast itself, with its notorious split personality: half efficient nanny, half wanton seductress. With all the psychological baggage a breast carries around, it's really no wonder that the sight of a breast-feeding infant provokes complex reactions, combining "Isn't that sweet?" with arousal, jealousy, disgust, or shame.

The fact that so few of us contemporary adults were nursed ourselves doesn't help much. Most of us saw our first bosom in a copy of *Playboy* filched from our father's night table and discovered nursing when our fifth-grade class took a trip to the farm. Eeww, we said, that's gross! Some of us haven't changed much since fifth grade.

In any case, nursing is in style again. Soon women will be nursing everywhere, and many more children will be nursed; finally we'll all get used to it and nobody will have to feel weird anymore. Not me, not you, and certainly not the babies, now drifting off to sleep with nipples half in, half out of their mouths, dreaming whatever babies dream.

Where Mommies Come From

have been pregnant five times. Two of these resulted in the little boys watching *Batman* in the next room, but this is mostly about the other three.

It was the autumn of my junior year in high school, just before the homecoming football game. Football games ordinarily came and went without my notice, but at the time I was in love with Alan Jacobson, who was in charge of the float our class was building for the half-time parade. I volunteered for the float committee just to hang around him and spent many cold nights in some cheerleader's garage, stuffing bits of crepe paper into chicken-wire sculptures of Dorothy, the Scarecrow, the Tin Man, and the Cowardly Lion.

One night there was an after-float-meeting party at

Alan's house, where I drank too much beer and finally was the only girl left. After I passed out in a hallway, some comedian put a hollow bear head over my face. I woke up half suffocating, disoriented, and sick, and barely made it to the blue-tiled bathroom. My next conscious moments were much later on, in Alan's bedroom after everyone was gone.

A few weeks later the time for my period came and went. I approached Alan at his locker before English class to give him the news.

Don't tell me, he said, tell Tim Turner.

Tim Turner was a guy I had been involved with a few months before. He had nothing to do with it. I went into the girls' room and cried all the way through English. Alan wouldn't help me; I was doomed. None of my girlfriends even had a driver's license, much less any money.

The next day I was sitting across from my mother at the big two-sided desk in her study, staring at my math homework. Tears started falling on the theorems and she asked what was wrong. Poor Mom. Drugs, shoplifting, hitchhiking, attempted suicide, now this.

Roe v. Wade was barely two years old at the time. In fact, I'd been on the eighth-grade debate team when legalized abortion rocketed into place alongside ecology and the school dress code as one of the most pressing issues of the day. I remember copying out the definition of D & C, dilation and curettage, into a three-ring binder. I wonder if schoolkids are doing that same sort of thing right now, looking up crack cocaine in the *Reader's Guide to Periodical Literature*.

There I was, the beneficiary of the new law I had so avidly defended. But if abortion had still been illegal, I'm sure my parents would have personally rowed me to Puerto Rico. A teenage pregnancy carried to term would ruin my schoolwork, my social life, my future: all more important to them than the two-week-old idea in my stomach. I was overwhelmed and heartbroken, and relieved to have someone else take charge.

Both my mother and my father accompanied me to the clinic on the appointed evening, their anger by then tempered with empathy. I had them pick me up at the float meeting because I wanted Alan (whom my father from this time on sarcastically referred to as Daddy) to guess what was going on. *See what you've done to me? Don't you care? Don't you care about me at all?* said the bitter look I flashed him as I waved good-bye and shuffled out to the car. Sandye followed me to the driveway and gave me a hug; no one else paid any attention.

There were other girls my age in the waiting room, but none of them were accompanied by their parents. Several had forlorn-looking boyfriends along, which I envied.

The next morning, I was back in school as usual. I walked the halls with my head down, surprised and almost angry that what had happened to me did not show. It was over, hardly anyone knew about it, and those who did never mentioned it again. Soon it was almost as if it had never happened.

Sometimes, alone at the bus stop or pacing around the empty football field after school, I let myself think about it. I'm sorry, I sobbed, wrapping my arms around my stomach. I'm so sorry.

My second pregnancy befell me four years later. I had just graduated from college and was up to my neck in a neurotic romance with Jan, a housemate from the co-op where I lived senior year. Our shared interests were filmmaking, hitchhiking, ninety-nine-cent breakfasts, and the destruction of the capitalist state. His previous love had been Squeaky Fromme, whom he still hoped to spring from jail.

By this point in my life I was certainly bright enough to use birth control, and did so. But I got pregnant anyway, a victim of imperfect technology. I missed a period while we were driving around the country in a beat-up Olds Cutlass, saying good-bye to all our friends before we left for our happy new life in Eastern Europe. Though I was sure I was pregnant, my tests came out negative in clinics from Saratoga to Las Vegas.

See, said Jan cheerfully as I slid into the car beside him, everything's fine.

Yeah, fine, I replied gloomily. I could just see myself three months later, wandering the streets of Dubrovnik, trying to find out the word for "abortion" in Serbo-Croatian.

When I got home, my mother took me to a doctor who insisted on giving me hormone pills to bring on my period. He said that I "couldn't be pregnant," and my mother, against all reason, seemed inclined to believe him. By the time the two of them wised up, I was scheduled to leave the country in a matter of days.

I had an abortion on the Fourth of July, with my long-suffering mother beside me; the doctor was in a hurry to get to a cookout. My socialist sweetheart did not manage to show up for the occasion.

Though I was still far from being mommy material, it was not easy to give up that baby. I knew that women younger than I, with less education and fewer resources, became mothers every day. Why not me? Well, why not? In my mind's eye, I held a darling little person with Jan's wire-rimmed glasses and bent nose. Please don't go, I thought, even as I lay on the doctor's steel table. Then the Valium drip and the cruel poking began.

As tragic as I felt, I knew I was lucky. Once again, the course of my life was not completely changed because of a dumb mistake.

During my twenties, the nesting instinct worked its wiles on me. I acquired an apartment, a mate, a respectable car, and a case of stroller lust. I want a baby, I said to the guy in my bed, and that was a sexy thing.

So Tony and I started trying to get me pregnant. "Trying" is the operative term here. As my past experience had shown, when one has no intention of having a baby, fertilization can scarcely be avoided. A tricky contraceptive device is just another thrilling challenge to the speedy young sperm with a dream. The traitorous ovum climbs out her window and sneaks down the tube to meet him. One might sooner try to prevent the full moon.

But once I'd become fascinated by the miracle of conception and was eager to try it out in my own home, things were suddenly more complex. I had to read books about breakthrough bleeding and cervical mucus, had to purchase basal thermometers and home pregnancy test kits. I had to have my IUD removed. By then they were illegal anyway. I was just waiting to get pulled over for an expired inspection sticker and have the cop stick his head in and ask, "I'm picking up something on the radar, miss. Not an illegal intrauterine device, I hope."

The minute my various predictive methods indicated that an egg had been produced by my ovary, we bombarded it with spermatozoa throughout its twelve- to twenty-four-hour lifespan, rushing home from work at lunch if possible.

This part was not exactly painful. More trying was the task of Quitting Everything. While I strongly suspected that my own mother had martinied and Marlboroed her way from the marital bed to the delivery table, and my sister and I were born whole nevertheless,

I was a woman of the just-say-no eighties. Cigarettes, alcohol, and recreational drugs were only the beginning of what I had to renounce. Caffeine, aspirin, permanent waves, and my beloved diet sodas were all to be abjured; I only thank God I didn't eat hot dogs, so I didn't have to stop.

I had always seen myself as fundamentally incorrigible. I believed in my obsessions and compulsions more than I believed in my ability to overcome them, or in any necessity to do so. Pick a vice, any vice: too much was never enough. I thought this a very romantic trait. Also essential to my persona was a certain recklessness. I would try anything, do anything—Egyptian cigars, horse tranquilizers, drag racing around town without seat belts in the middle of the night.

Now I had to turn the willfulness that had made me such an abandoned young decadent in the opposite direction. Since by this time I wanted to have a baby more than anything else, I did it.

So, fine. There I was with no hobbies, no pastimes, and little in common with anyone I knew, Tony foremost among them. Though at first I wept in frustration at parties where everyone was drinking and puffing, I gradually found I could have a good time anywhere, even with people who were totally looped. I developed preferences, noticing that people on cocaine talk your head off about matters of profound insignificance, whereas those who have taken psychedelics laugh so hard at your jokes that you soon believe you're ready to host a late-night talk show.

Ultimately, it all worked the way it was supposed to, and I was pregnant. I ate dark green vegetables, took vitamins, went to prenatal exercise class twice a week. We continued to pore over handbooks, guidebooks, and intrauterine photo essays, tracking the progress of our blob or blobette—whom we had by now nicknamed Pee-wee—through the forty weeks from pinhead to Pampers.

Sandye came down from New York to paint the nursery, an undersea dreamland with seahorses and starfish. We had three different bathtubs, piles of receiving blankets, a bassinet, a crib, clothes and washcloths and towels, a few carseats, dozens of stuffed animals, and what our friends at the shower described as the Porsche of strollers. We were signed up for diaper service and ready for action.

A few days before Peewee was due, I invited a mid-wife friend over for dinner. I wanted to talk labor. Even with all my studying, I was sure there was some vital secret I did not know. At this point, my stomach was so big I could hardly reach the countertop or bend to put the quiche in the oven.

Jenny asked me if I had been feeling any movement. I said I hadn't felt anything in a couple of days, but didn't babies tend to move less as they settled down into the pelvis right before birth? She said yes, but maybe she should go out to her car and get her bag so she could check the heart tones.

I lay down on my bed and she began to listen. As I watched her face, something deep inside me, some knowledge that I had been resisting, began to surface. I felt as if I were leaving my body, drifting out the window into the gray sky.

I called my doctor and left for the hospital, running back up the stairs to call Tony at the last minute. I so much didn't want to make that call that I almost forgot. Then, on the way there, we passed him in his green car, speeding down the street, looking grim and frightened. How can I do this to him? I thought. How can the universe do this to him? Just the day before he had washed and folded each tiny T-shirt and stacked them in the nursery closet.

At the hospital, my doctor confirmed that there was no heartbeat. The baby is dead, she said. She was crying.

Peewee was stillborn. Still, born. There was no explanation for what happened, not from the tiny, perfectly formed body I delivered the next day in the hospital, not from the autopsy that was performed after that. I remember holding him and thinking of the tightly curled bud of a flower whose petals will never open.

And the fun was not over yet. We had to go to a funeral home to make the arrangements. We had to make a million phone calls, tell a million people, open a mailbox full of sympathy cards every day. I had to take hormones to prevent my milk from coming in. My dead baby pills, I called them. The day after I stopped taking them, it came in anyway. I was sitting in a meeting at work when I saw the stain on my shirt.

I felt as if I had run at full speed with open arms into a brick wall. Every cell in my body, so ready to nurture my baby, ached with frustration and loneliness.

When a baby you want so badly is taken from you, it is hard to believe you ever gave one up by choice. In the crazy aftermath of Peewee's death, I brooded about bad karma. Three babies lost to me now, I thought, all lost. But I never really wished I had had those first two babies, or believed that I was damned for what I'd done.

Nor was I about to be thwarted by a mean universe. I shut the nursery door, got out my basal thermometer, and bought a pair of tickets to Puerto Vallarta. Two months later, I was pregnant again.

A couple of weeks before my thirtieth birthday, I had Hayes, a peaceful little baby with big ears and curious eyes, and tumbled headlong into the unbelievably wholesome and consuming experience of motherhood. I pureed carrots and peas, poured bleach into a plastic pail, sang old James Taylor songs over a skirted bassinet. And then I got really brave and had another, this time at home, with a midwife, in my very own bed. My sister, Nancy, came down to watch. Holy shit, she said, as Vincent emerged from between my legs.

*   *   *

I am not the greatest mother on earth, though I am a hell of a lot better than I would have been at sixteen or twenty. I don't have very much patience, and there are still a lot of things I want to do in a day besides make sandwiches and search for matching socks and drive to and from the Montessori school and play Candyland. I yell too much, I bribe them with sweets, and sometimes I just want to run away. But I don't. I love them, and I asked for this. I prayed for it.

There is only so much choice to be had in this world. I think we need as much as we can get.

Secrets of the Natives

My friend Sandye would say that in the South, at least, "summer fun" is an oxymoron, like "jumbo shrimp." But Sandye is the type of person who thinks air-conditioning is a moral issue. When she rented a house with a window unit, she pushed it out into the yard and left it to rust. Then she lay on the couch all summer with the heat on top of her like a sweaty lover. In September she rolled him off and got into the car.

Is fun all you care about? a serious-minded boyfriend once asked. Yes! I said, opening a bottle of champagne. This guy had to think meaningful thoughts and engage in productive activities all day long. He wanted to sleep at night and go to work in the morning. Back then, this attitude drove me mad. I left him and the action-crazed northern city he lived in and headed for the latitudes of lassitude that were my soul's hometown.

To me, the southern summer has a spacey off-season quality, as in a resort town that reserves certain pleasures for year-round residents. Such as idling at a four-way stop sign, sipping a Thirstbuster, twisting the dial on the radio until you find the perfect song. Escaping the infinite afternoon in the velvet icebox of an empty cinema, seeing something that floats across your eyes without disturbing your brain. That dizzy moment at the end when you exit through the fire door and the heat actually feels good on your chilled skin.

How the mercury rises slowly, how the morning clouds burn off, and suddenly the sky is blue on blue. All day it goes on like that, hotter and hotter, bluer and bluer, until armpits are sticky, tempers are short, and fortunately the cocktail hour is at hand. There are few things wrong with summer that an ice-cold beer can't cure. To say nothing of a frozen margarita. Indolence, indulgence, intoxication: this is the general progression. Having abandoned the self-improvement programs so resolutely adopted at New Year's, having quarreled with the gentle lovers of spring, a drunken interlude with a stranger is to be expected.

At home, however, our private parts are unenergetic. We take cold showers, then sit in front of the fan. Clothes hang limp in the closet; exercise bikes rust from disuse; only the plastic ice trays flex like Hungarian gymnasts, ice cubes flying twelve at a time into oversized cups. In a burst of iced-tea-related energy, we dash off an SOS to the advice columnist of the local paper. The bugs again, of course—what else is there? Per her suggestion, we sprinkle garlic and brewer's yeast and borax and sugar and Sevin-dust all over the house and garden, and our dog develops a persistent little cough.

We don't bake, or broil, or use flashbulbs. At parties, we serve favorite foods from the hottest places on earth: gazpacho, tabouli, ceviche, Long Island iced tea. We buy peaches from the peach truck and watermelon from the watermelon truck and eat corn that was picked today, just before dawn. These tomatoes have never had any rain on them, the old farmer said, as if they were precious virgins. And we have been loving those tomatoes all week long.

We make plans for future summers, playing backgammon in a bungalow on Nantucket, wearing sailor suits in France, eating blackberries on an island in the Northwest. In the meantime, we cultivate friends with pools and boats. We love our friends, and we spend a good deal of time with them. We call them on the phone and speak to them hopefully, our cheeks slightly damp against the receiver.

We spread our towels on cement at the city pool, reading book reviews instead of books. Then the newsprint heats up, and the ink comes off on our hands. Everything is yellow, a little girl in the shallow end is shouting. My house is yellow that umbrella is yellow the water is yellow you're yellow I'm yellow the sky is yellow. No one corrects her. Obviously she is right.

Going Out to Breakfast, and Other Grounds for Divorce

t was not yet dawn when the baby crawled on top of me and started sucking my chin. I reached for the clock, saw it was just after six, rearranged him into a sleeping position, and rolled over. In the process, I awakened his father.

Where you going? mumbled Tony.

Nowhere, I said. This proved to be inaccurate, as the baby popped up again with a brilliant smile, indicating that as far as he was concerned, the day had begun.

Well, I thought, if we all have to be up a whole hour earlier than necessary, we may as well make the best of it. Why don't we go out to breakfast? I suggested.

What time is it? asked Tony, disbelieving.

Around six.

Oh . . . okay. Where should we go?

I don't know, what's open?

He yawned, Kerbey Lane, Omelettry, Mongolian Café . . . they're all probably open by now.

By Mongolian Café I assumed he meant the nearby Magnolia Café, but I could hardly believe he had suggested it, knowing how much he hated the oversized and undercooked home fries, the "old hippie" atmosphere, the crowded-together tables with their vinyl-covered Guatemalan-blanket tablecloths. Or could he possibly be talking about the Mongolian Barbecue out in Oak Hill? Somehow I couldn't picture us driving ten miles to eat stir-fried pork for breakfast.

In any case, I did not immediately pick up on any of his suggestions. What self-respecting married person would? How about Las Manitas? I suggested.

See if they're open, he said.

The phone at Las Manitas was answered with a sleepy *Bueno*. I hesitated for a second. It was kind of early for foreign phrases. *A qué hora está abierto?* I ventured.

Seven-thirty, said the Las Manitan, in English.

I reported this information. Seven-thirty was an hour away and I had to be at work by eight, so Las Manitas was really out of the question.

How about Trudy's? he asked.

Original or south? I replied, knowing full well that he abhorred one and I disliked the other.

So the deliberations began. I picked up the soaking-wet baby and headed down the hall to infant headquarters. While doing so, I decided that there were three important criteria for selecting a breakfast venue. First, we should go somewhere close to the house so we could take one car and I could drop the two of them back at the house on my way to work. Second, decent decaffeinated coffee. Third, oatmeal for the baby.

When I returned to the bedroom, Tony was still under the covers. Seis Salsas? he suggested before I could speak.

Since this was one of our favorite restaurants, it should have been a reasonable proposal. However, it didn't meet a single one of my as-yet-undivulged criteria. Nah, I said.

What I would really like, he replied, is some fresh-squeezed juice.

Fresh-squeezed juice? This was trouble. I couldn't think of anywhere nearby that had fresh-squeezed juice *and* oatmeal. By now it was seven o'clock. Let's just go to the Magnolia, I said, it's our best bet.

I hate the Magnolia Café, he countered testily.

Why? I asked innocently.

You know why! Why do you always want to go to the one restaurant I don't like?

You're the one who suggested it in the first place. I never would have even brought it up.

I was kidding, he shouted.

Maybe Las Manitas is open by now, I said wearily. I called them again, but they still opened at seven-thirty.

The novelty of going out to breakfast in the dark was fading fast. More bickering ensued. Names of increasingly improbable restaurants were bandied about. At seven-fifteen, we left for Las Manitas.

We'd better take two cars, I said grimly.

As I dressed, I thought fondly of the Magnolia Café. I saw the three of us sitting in a booth by the window, morning light pooling on the vinyl tabletop. My steaming cup, full of delicious decaf. I would order the Economical: two eggs, toast, and potatoes. For once the home fries would be perfect. But no. We couldn't go there, not today, not ever! It was too unfair! We were totally incompatible, that's all there was to it.

Tony had the baby and was waiting with his coat on by the door, car keys in hand. Oh, let's just take one car, I said, trying to make amends.

God damn it, he yelled, throwing his keys across the room. Can't you ever make up your mind about anything?

Once a marital spat has begun, it's so difficult to end. One person's olive branch is the other's stupid broken stick.

I'm sorry! Jesus Christ! Let's just go!

The baby, unfazed by his grumpy parents, joyfully waved good-bye to no one in particular.

In the car, I began to fully experience the pathos of our situation. I pictured us in the early days of our romance, awakening early—say ten-thirty—and lazily deciding to go out to eat. We would end up at some

favorite place without even having to discuss it. We'd
share an omelette, then smoke cigarettes from the same
pack. Now we didn't even smoke anymore, or at least
only behind each other's back, and then we favored
different brands. What was next, I wondered. Twin
beds? Separate vacations?

Oh, I sighed, we're a couple of old farts. A second
olive branch.

Speak for yourself, grumbled the man in the passen-
ger seat.

Fuck you, I grumbled back.

Watch your driving. There's a baby in the car.

I looked in the rearview mirror and saw he was right.
There *was* a baby in the car. It was still a little hard to
believe.

The remainder of the drive to Las Manitas was com-
pleted in silence. At the restaurant, we stared blankly at
the menu. Even before we spoke, our waiter could sense
that this was not a happy table.

I'll have orange juice, said Tony.

I'll have carrot juice, said I.

Oh, I'm sorry, said the waiter. We just opened. It'll
be a while before the juice is ready.

What do you mean, a while? Ten minutes? Half an
hour? By lunchtime? I was losing it.

The waiter rolled his eyes. I'll bring you some as
soon as it's squeezed, he said. Would you like something to eat? Some coffee?

Huevos rancheros and decaf for me, I said.

I'll have *migas* and coffee, said Tony.

Migas con queso? asked the waiter.

No, no cheese.

The waiter looked confused. I decided to help out. They don't have *migas* with no cheese, honey. They have with cheese, or with cheese and mushrooms. No cheese isn't a choice.

Tony threw down his menu in despair.

You want something without cheese? I asked helpfully. Get *huevos mexicanos*.

I don't care, he mumbled. I'm not hungry.

Bring him the *huevos mexicanos*, I said. The waiter was deserting us as I spoke. And some extra flour tortillas!

Just then, a waitress finished writing the specials on the board.

Chilaquiles! moaned Tony. I should have had *chilaquiles*.

But *chilaquiles* has tons of cheese! I thought you didn't want cheese.

I didn't, he muttered.

After six years, he was still an enigma.

Our son, meanwhile, was up to his usual restaurant antics, scattering silverware and Sweet'n Low, trying to drink the hot sauce, knocking over a full glass of water. And no oatmeal to keep him occupied. I sighed and went in search of a high chair.

The food came quickly, thank God, and was flawless, thank God, though we didn't have much time to linger over it. At this point, I was already late for work. The perfect ending to the perfect fiasco.

Then on the way home, Tony reached over and touched my hand on the gearshift.

We should do this more often, he said.

Yeah, right, I snorted.

No, I mean it, he insisted.

Now there was an olive branch with my name on it. Should I accept?

Ya ya ya ya ya, said the baby in the backseat, and I took his advice.

What Are Friends For?

was thinking about how everybody can't be everything to each other, but some people can be something to each other, thank God, from the ones whose shoulder you cry on to the ones whose half-slips you borrow to the nameless ones you chat with in the grocery line.

Buddies, for example, are the workhorses of the friendship world, the people out there on the front lines, defending you from loneliness and boredom. They call you up, they listen to your complaints, they celebrate your successes and curse your misfortunes, and you do the same for them in return. They hold out through innumerable crises before concluding that the person you're dating is no good, and even then understand if you ignore their good counsel. They accompany you to a movie with subtitles or to see the diving pig at Aquarena Springs. They feed your cat when you are out of town and pick you up from the airport when you get back. They come over to help you decide what to wear on a date. Even if it is with that creep.

What about family members? Most of them are people you just got stuck with, and though you love them, you may not have very much in common. But there is that rare exception, the Relative Friend. It is your cousin, your brother, maybe even your aunt. The two of you share the same views of the other family members. Meg never should have divorced Martin. He was the best thing that ever happened to her. You can confirm each other's memories of things that happened a long time ago. Don't you remember when Uncle Hank and Daddy had that awful fight in the middle of Thanksgiving dinner? Grandma always hated Grandpa's stamp collection; she probably left the windows open during the hurricane on purpose.

While so many family relationships are tinged with guilt and obligation, a relationship with a Relative Friend is relatively worry-free. You don't even have to hide your vices from this delightful person. When you slip out Aunt Joan's back door for a cigarette, she is already there.

Then there is that special guy at work. Like all the other people at the job site, at first he's just part of the scenery. But gradually he starts to stand out from the crowd. Your friendship is cemented by jokes about co-workers and thoughtful favors around the office. Did you see Ryan's hair? Want half my bagel?

Soon you know the names of his turtles, what he did last Friday night, exactly which model CD player he wants for his birthday. His handwriting is as familiar to you as your own.

Though you invite each other to parties, you somehow don't quite fit into each other's outside lives. For this reason, the friendship may not survive a job change. Company gossip, once an infallible source of entertainment, soon awkwardly accentuates the distance between you. But wait. Like School Friends, Work Friends share certain memories which acquire a nostalgic glow after about a decade.

A Faraway Friend is someone you grew up with or went to school with or lived in the same town as until one of you moved away. Without a Faraway Friend, you would never get any mail addressed in handwriting. A Faraway Friend calls late at night, invites you to her wedding, always says she is coming to visit but rarely shows up. An actual visit from a Faraway Friend is a cause for celebration and binges of all kinds. Cigarettes, Chips Ahoy, bottles of tequila.

Faraway Friends go through phases of intense communication, then may be out of touch for many months. Either way, the connection is always there. A conversation with your Faraway Friend always helps to put your life in perspective: when you feel you've hit a dead end, come to a confusing fork in the road, or gotten lost in some crackerbox subdivision of your life, the advice of the Faraway Friend—who has the big picture, who is so well acquainted with the route that brought you to this place—is indispensable.

Another useful function of the Faraway Friend is to help you remember things from a long time ago, like the name of your seventh-grade history teacher, what was in that really good stir-fry, or exactly what happened that night on the boat with the guys from Florida.

Ah, the Former Friend. A sad thing. At best a wistful memory, at worst a dangerous enemy who is in possession of many of your deepest secrets. But what was it that drove you apart? A misunderstanding, a betrayed confidence, an unrepaid loan, an ill-conceived flirtation. A poor choice of spouse can do in a friendship just like that. Going into business together can be a serious mistake. Time, money, distance, cult religions: all noted friendship killers. You quit doing drugs, you're not such good friends with your dealer anymore.

And lest we forget, there are the Friends You Love to Hate. They call at inopportune times. They say stupid things. They butt in, they boss you around, they embarrass you in public. They invite themselves over. They take advantage. You've done the best you can, but they need professional help. On top of all this, they love you to death and are convinced they're your best friend on the planet.

So why do you continue to be involved with these people? Why do you tolerate them? On the contrary, the real question is, What would you do without them? Without Friends You Love to Hate, there would be nothing to talk about with your other friends. Their problems and their irritating stunts provide a reliable source of conversation for everyone they know. What's more, Friends You Love to Hate make you feel good about yourself, since you are obviously in so much better shape than they are. No matter what these people do, you will never get rid of them. As much as they need you, you need them too.

At the other end of the spectrum are Hero Friends. These people are better than the rest of us, that's all there is to it. Their career is something you wanted to be when you grew up—painter, forest ranger, tireless doer of good. They have beautiful homes filled with special handmade things presented to them by villagers in the remote areas they have visited in their extensive travels. Yet they are modest. They never gossip. They are always helping others, especially those who have suffered a death in the family or an illness. You would think people like this would just make you sick, but somehow they don't.

A New Friend is a tonic unlike any other. Say you meet her at a party. In your bowling league. At a Japanese conversation class, perhaps. Wherever, whenever, there's that spark of recognition. The first time you talk, you can't believe how much you have in common. Suddenly, your life story is interesting again, your insights fresh, your opinion valued. Your various shortcomings are as yet completely invisible.

It's almost like falling in love.

Houseguest Heaven and Hell

Me, I like to feed people and find them extra blankets and turn on the light so they won't try to read in the dark. I like to know what everyone's doing, and when, and with whom, and I don't mind giving out a little friendly advice. I can organize impromptu activities with my hands tied behind my back. I should have been a mother superior, or a cruise director.

With a houseful of houseguests, I'm in my element. Even obligatory daily routines like cooking dinner or going to the store take on a festive air when there's company in the house. With the right houseguests, you have an extended family, a commune, a tribe. But unlike your real family or housemates or tribespeople, the visitors are not permanent. All the more reason to enjoy.

I remember reading somewhere that a good Christian treats every guest at his door as if he or she might be

Jesus Christ. I don't go that far. I do supply a clean towel, a cup of coffee in the morning, and my video club membership card. Don't make long-distance calls on my telephone, don't leave lights on in rooms not in use, help with the dishes once in a while, and we'll get along fine.

If you lined up end to end all the people who have ever slept under my roof, you wouldn't quite have House-guests Across America. Across Belize, maybe. About half of them would be old boyfriends and relatives and schoolmates and the other half I wouldn't even recognize. Friends of friends of not such good friends, people I met for maybe half an hour on a train, somebody who knew the girl who lived in this place before us, could he please stay here for just one night?

In this very long line of houseguests with their feet in each other's faces, there are both shining examples of the species and their evil twins, the houseguests from hell. There's no easy way to tell them apart when they first show up on your doorstep, all smiles and courtesy and preemptive gratitude. But gradually the trouble-makers give themselves away, usually with certain un-mistakable portents.

They arrive unannounced, often in parties of two or more. Temporarily between addresses, they have strapped everything they own to the roof of their car or stuffed it into the trunk—at least whatever they didn't sell in the yard sale back where they came from, Oak-land or Lake Charles or somewhere. They're just stopping in to visit on the way to . . . now where is it they said they were going? No one seems to recall that either. Perhaps they have some unspecified "business" here in town. In any case, within the first few days, their car expires in your driveway.

They drink too much or smoke too much or perhaps are not quite recovered from a recent illness, physical or mental. A formidable number of prescription pill bottles appear beside the bed. Each guest corners you to explain confidentially about the others. She has a little problem, you see. He's not well.

After a week or two, their pots, pans, toilet items, appliances, dishes, clothes, and knickknacks have been unloaded onto your front porch and are making their way into the house. You're living in your bedroom with the door shut, trying to avoid them. You stop buying food, leaving them to live on white bread and the case of brown gravy mix they brought along. They pawn their toaster oven to buy port and Coca-Cola.

They know you want them to leave, that much is sure, but they have no money and no place to go. They are definitely making long-distance phone calls. You bring it up gently, but they are haughty and offended, insisting the calls were collect. Later you overhear a whispered conversation in which you are referred to as "that bitch."

They fail to leave as they arrived, en masse; instead, they dwindle away one at a time. For the last straggler, you have to buy a bus ticket to the next destination, where he claims to have friends anxiously awaiting his arrival. He demands to be taken to the station the night before his six A.M. departure. Take me now, he says coldly. I won't trouble you a moment longer. You leave him sitting stiffly in the deserted terminal.

All night long, you toss and turn, half expecting a call. At six A.M., you sigh with relief and pour yourself a glass of port and Coke.

At six-thirty, the phone rings. The bus was oversold; they asked for volunteers to get off. Have you ever heard of that happening with a bus? And there isn't another departure until that evening. You've learned your lesson; you bring over a sack lunch.

You have a surprisingly successful garage sale with the stuff they left behind. Maybe people are pickier in Lake Charles. Years later, you are still finding brown gravy packets in the oddest places.

A common trait of bad houseguests is that they take up too much space, physically and psychically. They spread out, they rearrange, they encroach. One day while you are at work, they silk-screen political slogans on your front door, as did my college boyfriend Jan when he dropped in for a few weeks during Impeach Reagan mania. He was not the type to think about a petty matter like a security deposit. One time, Scott and Lexanne found a huge cardboard box of mildewed marijuana in their laundry closet after bidding farewell to a shady character who spent his postdivorce depression in their care.

Then there is the loudmouth hyperactive houseguest who bosses you around, flirts with your boyfriend, makes fun of the contents of your refrigerator. She whips up a quiche in the pan you usually use to clean out the aquarium and you do not tell her. She has sex in your downstairs bathroom and in the process tears the sink off the wall. Sad to confess, these last are sins of my own.

I really do believe in hospitality, so it's a pleasure to exercise it on behalf of the deserving. Among many fondly remembered visitors to my home, the class of the field are Shelley and Pete, a printmaker and a musician who live outside the log flume of society in which the rest of us bump and barrel along. They have no permanent address, no telephone, no jobs, very little money. These are not your ordinary overnighters. They're professionals. Career houseguests. They drive around the country in an old Buick Wildcat, heading south in the winter and back north in the summer, connecting the dots between their friends' addresses. Well-worn though their welcome may be, it is in no danger of wearing out. No one's anything but glad when they pull up in the driveway, and anything but sorry to see them go. So what's their secret? How have they won the hearts of hosts from coast to coast?

First, they are very relaxed. They don't want to go to the state capitol, the mall, and the botanical gardens, all before having lunch by the river. They like to do things you would want to do anyway, like rent a movie, call out for pizza, or go down to the bar on the corner for a beer. If they want to do something you're not interested in, they just go ahead and do it themselves. Or you can go out and leave them home. They'll sit at your kitchen table and drink a beer or ten and still be sitting there chitchatting when you return. They have their own car, and they have each other, which gives them quite an edge.

Another advantage is their compact size. A narrow couch is more than spacious enough to sleep both. And while some guests take over your house with valises and tote bags and piles of papers, Shelley and Pete seem to have no stuff at all. Maybe they leave it all out in the car.

Though their means are slender, they are never broke. They always pay their share at restaurants and bars, insist on chipping in for groceries, and keep your refrigerator stocked with beer at all times. Somehow those twelve cans of Schaefer make every day seem like Friday. And they don't take forty-five-minute showers when you are trying to get ready for work; in fact, they don't take many showers at all. But they don't smell, which is more than I can say for some who have crossed my portals. Hogar, if you're reading this, change your socks.

They are helpful like you cannot believe. They walk the dog, keep an eye on the kids, have a pot of red beans and rice on the stove when you get home from work. They unclog the disposal, fix the birdhouse, paint the porch, run down to the store; you can't pay people to do half the stuff they do.

Finally, they know, no matter what you say, that one day you'll start to want your house back to yourself. But that day never dawns because they know when to leave. Which is always before you're ready to see them go. You try to talk them into staying, but they won't give in.

And so you stand on the porch, waving good-bye, then go in to straighten the guest room. As usual, the houseguests have left something behind: a paperback book, perhaps, or a copper bracelet. It's a signal, as clear as a new lover's socks found tangled in the sheets the next afternoon.

They'll be back.

A Very Good Friday Indeed

t was Unremarkable Thursday. I was at my desk at the software company, slapping together a newsletter to hand out at a trade show the following week, making phone calls, conducting interviews with happy customers, sending faxes, writing articles, getting bids from printers. It was late in the day, and everyone I spoke with seemed to be on his or her way out the door and wouldn't be in until Monday, or in some cases Tuesday. Why? Tomorrow is Good Friday, someone explained, and Sunday is Easter. Monday was something else, I don't remember what. As far as I knew, my company wasn't closed for Good Friday, or Wonderful Monday either. We certainly never had been in the past.

But how was I going to get this newsletter done if everyone I needed to talk to was gone until next week? I typed and dialed and talked and drank coffee faster and faster. Then my friend Denise stopped by my office and said, Hey, what are you doing tomorrow?

Working on this damn newsletter, I said.

But we're closed tomorrow.

Nah, I said.

Yes, we are, she persisted.

Really? I said. Are you sure?

Though the firm had once been too small even to have an official list of holidays, we had grown quite a bit over the last year. I recalled having received a memo on the subject some time ago and rummaged through my drawer to unearth it. My God, she was right.

I slowly hung up the phone, pushed back my keyboard, unclenched my mouse, and eyed the piles of papers and phone messages that surrounded me. Hard as it was to believe, I had tomorrow off. It was already after five. But could I just leave my newsletter in this half-baked condition? Would I have time to finish it if I waited until Monday?

I never forgot about anything so fast in my life.

Tomorrow off! I could hardly believe my good fortune. The calendar had screeched to a halt between scheduled stops, the doors slid smoothly open, and I found myself standing in tall green grass at the edge of the world.

Real time off, time completely free from structure and obligation, is a rare and blissful thing. Though major holidays, vacations, and weekends may appear to qualify, they all have characteristics that can hinder the pure experience of time-off mind. The Thanksgiving–Hanukkah–Christmas–New Year omnibus is jammed with social and family functions, religious rituals, and trips to the mall, heralded by preholiday stress and trailed by postholiday depression. Even if you don't jump on the bandwagon and kill yourself, you hardly feel that your time is your own.

The summertime civic occasions—Memorial Day, the Fourth, and Labor Day—have their own mandatory observances. You have to spend the whole day watching or participating in sports, drinking beer, eating potato salad, and being eaten in turn by mosquitoes, often with people you don't really like but have been spending this day with every year since the dawn of time. Honey, you say to your partner in life on the way home in the car, can't we do something else next year? Sure, he or she says. I'd love to. Three hundred and sixty-five days later, there you are again. Fortunately these holidays are scheduled so that they create a shortened workweek, giving them some redeeming value.

Planning and taking a vacation can be a part-time job in itself. A destination must be selected, money saved, transportation arranged, bags packed, pet care provided for, elaborate lighting schemes to deter potential intruders devised, safe aviation and cooperative weather fretted over. Then the trip is over before you know it and you need another week off to recover.

Weekends are okay but unreasonably short. What with all the chores and errands and extra-thick newspapers and recreational activities, it's suddenly Sunday night and you're exhausted.

A really perfect day off has to sneak up on you from behind, like Presidents' Day or Columbus Day, Good Friday if you're not a good Christian, Rosh Hashanah for all but good Jews (Rush-a-Home-a, I once overheard a black man on a New York bus call it). Or a day when nature cancels all our plans in one fell swoop, with a flood or a power failure or a snowstorm. As long as the disaster is not too disastrous, such days have the thrilling quality of life in wartime: listening for bulletins on the radio, searching for candles and checking provisions, playing cards, talking to strangers, pitching in to help.

Even a sick day can be spiritually replenishing if you're not too ill to enjoy it, not so busy that you have to feel guilty, and don't have small children in the house. Everyone leaves for school or work and the neighborhood is quiet, a placid map of empty streets and driveways. You watch a talk show, have a piece of toast, fall back to sleep. Go to the bathroom a lot. Wear sweatpants all day. Make a desultory search for the bouillon cubes. Look at a magazine, read the same paragraph half a dozen times. Fall into a languorous swoon waiting for the mailman. Someone calls at three to see if you're all right. Did I wake you? Mmmm.

* * *

Just barely awake, I feel Good Friday open before me like a flower, concave and welcoming, I can't see the end. Not for a moment do I mistake this day for some other, when the cold hands of the alarm clock drag me out of bed and it takes all the superego I can muster not to resist. Today the hours will run together like the miles of a Texas highway, sunny and undifferentiated, motionless and moving, unbroken by road signs and time clocks into compartments of impatience.

I lie in bed imagining all the things I might accomplish. I guess I could convert, go to church, and think about the Crucifixion, but it seems a little late for that. (Why *do* they call it "Good" Friday, anyway?) If some sort of penance is in order, I could clean my closets, or perhaps do my taxes.

Read a novel? Write some letters? For at least a while, I'll just lie here and consider the possibilities as the thin shadows of the venetian blinds move across the bed. Whatever I do, I will do slowly and with great pleasure, for today is Most Excellent Friday and all of it is mine.

Work: The Early Years

By the summer of my tenth year, I had had it with tag and spud and hide-and-go-seek. Sleep-away camp, I knew, was just a front for humiliation of the uncoordinated. With enough sun and fun under my belt to last me through puberty, I was chafing at the bit, ready for real life—a summer job. In terms of glamour and sophistication, slaving for a paycheck seemed right up there with having a boyfriend and smoking cigarettes.

Still too young for working papers, I founded a corporation with my sister, Nancy, and our next-to-next-door neighbor, Carolyn Mahoney. Manaca, we called it, combining the first syllables of our first names. Manaca was in the business of manufacturing and selling jars of colored water. Our wide array of tints was achieved by a proprietary process of marinating Magic Markers in club soda, and our containers ran from top-of-the-line selections like a lidded goblet that had once contained bath oil beads to a simple but elegant mayonnaise jar.

I was the president, Nancy was the secretary, Carolyn was the maid. My sister and I had been well trained by our mother. In every pursuit, when it came time to hand out roles, we always made sure there was a maid. And it was never either of us. Even when we played Time Tunnel, based on our favorite TV show, we had a Doug, a Tony, an Ann, and a maid. But there is no maid on *Time Tunnel*, Carolyn complained. Shut up and scrub the jungle gym, we told her.

By the summer of '68, we were not interested in mindless fun like Time Tunnel. We played school and office and store, we made rules and elected officers, sold shares, collected dues, and took inventory. Best of all were activities where actual money could be made. Any fool could see the lemonade-stand approach was not going to work on our suburban street, where no cars or people with money went by all day long. So Manaca was born, designed with the homebound housewife in mind. Like junior Avon ladies or renegade Girl Scouts, we produced an illustrated catalog and went door to door.

One of our jars, a rather plain smallish bottle containing royal blue water, became a sentimental favorite. We christened it Columbus and vowed it would never be sold. We put Columbus in a place of honor in our clubhouse, and rode our bikes in crazy circles around him, shouting, Don't knock over Columbus.

Manaca did a booming business until Daniel Malachowsky, a little boy down the street who was either
slightly retarded or perhaps just partially deaf, we never
really knew, sneaked into our playhouse and smashed
Columbus. We wreaked our evil-little-girl revenge—
equal parts screeching, jeering, and outlandish threats
of mayhem—which resulted in the corporation's being
forced to dissolve by parental decree. We saved the
pieces of glass that were once Columbus in a box.

By the time the colored-water business dried up, I
was twelve, old enough for the coveted career of babysitter. Three afternoons a week, I took the school bus to an
apartment complex near my house, where I sat for an
affable one-year-old named J.J. I changed J.J.'s diaper
and fixed his bottle of juice, and then we settled down
to watch *Dark Shadows*. As was the custom for babysitters, I ate his family out of house and home.

The following year I graduated to mother's helper,
basically no more than a full-time babysitting position.
Having spent many summers under the supervision of
ditzy preteens myself, I knew exactly what this employment involved. You got dropped off at the beach with
the kids and a sack of cheese sandwiches. They ran wild
with their friends while you lolled around on chaise
longues with the other mother's helpers, swooning over
magazines and lifeguards. This paid about twenty-five
cents an hour, which seemed fair enough.

The day I turned fourteen, minimum wage was mine.
Just let anyone try to offer me less than a dollar and a

quarter per hour. I was so excited that I took two jobs. I worked breakfast and lunch at a coffee shop on the boardwalk and sold tickets at the U-Pedal boat ride in the evening. My mother took me to the uniform store to get fitted for my very own white polyester dress and black apron. In the window, shapely mannequins displayed new fashions for cleaning ladies and nurses. A heavyset black lady took my measurements with a tape. Get you some good shoes, honey, she advised.

However, our main activity at the coffee shop was not carrying heavy trays but crouching behind the counter stuffing our faces. We were allowed one meal during our shift; that we ordered right after punching in. A half hour later we'd write up fake orders for chocolate chip pancakes, loading them with ice cream, strawberries, and whipped topping and stashing them on a shelf below the counter. When the bell on the front door jingled as a customer came in, we'd poke our heads up from our plates, peering between the pie cases to see whose section they chose. It was best to stop chewing before you asked for their order.

At three-thirty, I walked down the boardwalk to my second shift. The U-Pedal boats were owned by a golf partner of my father's, staffed by his oldest son, Howie Schwartz, and Howie's cute high school friends. This was like having my own private crew of lifeguards. *I Like Mike but I'm Partial to Marshall*, I wrote in my diary. While embezzling at the coffee shop was limited to food items, the U-Pedal boats offered much more

lucrative possibilities. The tickets were numbered so
Schwartz senior could check the number of tickets sold
against the amount in the cash box. The guys who ran
the rides would bring me back the tickets they had just
collected from the customers, and I would sell them
again. After work, we'd count up the extra money and
someone with fake ID would go buy beer. We drank it
under the stars on the top deck of the ticket boat, lying
on the indoor-outdoor carpeting.

Some nights I would go with Howie and a few of the
others to their Guru Maharaj Ji meetings, where somebody played guitar and they sang a song to the tune of
"This Land Is Your Land" with lyrics about the fourteen-
year-old perfect master. They burned incense and ate
plates of curried cauliflower. I never quite saw the ap-
peal. I preferred to meet my sister at Lee's pinball parlor,
where we would play Aquarius and Sheriff, then hang out
on a certain bench on the boardwalk where the cruelest,
most beautiful teenage hoodlums were sure to be.

The next summer I turned my back on the amoral
twilight world of the boardwalk and went to work in my
father's office in New York City. Commuting back and
forth in the car each day was probably the most time I
had ever spent alone with my father. We would wait in
traffic jams, then wait at tollbooths, then wait for the
parking-garage elevator. By the time we got to the street,
my father was about to explode from forced inertia. I
hurried along behind him three long blocks and one
short one, smelling newspapers and sidewalks and sub-

way trains, avoiding the occasional rolling clothes rack of a garment-district delivery boy.

Everyone at my father's office was very kind to me. My friend in the file room taught me to drink coffee and to fix runs in my pantyhose with nail polish. Some days I got to run the switchboard, which was my favorite job, plugging and unplugging the hydra of trunk lines into the slots until there was a mass of tangled wires and I was disconnecting people right and left. We answered the phone in the old-fashioned style, no greeting, just the last four digits of the number. Oh-five-one-oh, one moment, please, oh-five-one-oh. I affected a Brooklyn accent when I did this. After I flirted with the elevator boy all summer, he came down to Jersey to see me one Saturday night. What do you mean you don't want to, he moaned. I drove all duh way down heah from Queens. Later, he wrote me horny letters from the army.

My last job before I went off to college was at the law firm of Klitzman, Klitzman, Goldstein, and Gallagher. Given my impressive New York switchboard experience, they started me out as a receptionist. Here we answered the phone by saying "Klitzman, Klitzman, Goldstein, and Gallagher, may I help you?" This was not easy to do without cracking up. Finally I was transferred to the file department, a setting straight out of Kafka, with tottering piles of paper everywhere, legal parchments and packets, accordion files of writs and contracts and letters, black-and-white photographs of crime scenes and victims. Particularly difficult to file

were the close-up shots of things like wounds or potholes, tossed into our in-tray with no further identifica-
tion. The two other clerks and I worked like maniacs,
filing, misfiling, sometimes just throwing things away,
but no matter what we did, the windswept stacks con-
tinually grew. Even after a case had been settled, the
production of paper related to it continued unabated.

The winter after I left the Klitzman empire, a fire
burned the office and all its files to the ground. I found
this somehow heartening. By then I was in college, the
minimum wage was two dollars and thirty cents, and
work was never so good or so stupid again.

Meditations on a Stolen Purse

As part of an endless series of handbag-related disasters in my life, the most beautiful purse in the world was stolen from my car while it was parked outside my condo on my friendly street in my quiet neighborhood in Yuppieville, U.S.A. Someone strolled into the parking lot, saw a purse under my dash, opened the door, took it, and left. This happened on a sunny Thursday afternoon with me sitting in my living room not ten yards away.

When I first saw it wasn't in the car, I thought, Hmmm, must have left it in the house. When a quick search of the house yielded nothing, I thought, Hmmm, better take another look in the car. I went on like this, not the least bit worried, until the next day. When it was time to go to work, and I went to find my purse, and frantic rummagings through closets, under couches, in the freezer, through the laundry basket, and back out in the car proved fruitless, I began to realize the awful truth: I would never see the most beautiful purse in the world again.

I hesitate to describe it, for I know I can't do it justice. If I had to guess, I'd say it was a souvenir from the gift shop at Yellowstone Park circa 1953. It was hand-tooled, hand-stitched leather decorated with bison and deer and elk, sky and grass and mountains, blue and green and brown and white. It had two short wooden handles, also covered in leather, and was lined with soft brown moiré. Okay, now, whatever you're picturing, it was twenty times more beautiful. Plus the lady at the store gave it to me for eight dollars off the marked price. Life could not have been more sweet. I transferred everything out of my boring old purse into my beautiful new purse before I even left the store.

Five short days later, it was gone. No ransom note, no footprints, no trail of bobby pins, no response to the signs I tacked up around the neighborhood. HANDSOME REWARD FOR BEAUTIFUL PURSE, they proclaimed.

Okay, I admit it. My car wasn't locked. But I was only going upstairs for a minute. Okay, an hour. Okay, two hours and forty-five minutes. Okay, I was asking for it. That doesn't help.

The problem is, you want to feel safe. You don't want to think that you live in a world where crazy, bad people do stupid, cruel things. That every once in a while your number comes up, you're the victim of this random badness, and just like that, something you love is gone. If you're lucky, it's only a purse. At first, you can't stop seeing the lost things in your mind's eye. The little gold clasp. The dog-eared business card stuck in the inside pocket. The alligator checkbook case. The Scarlet Moon lipstick (a shade since discontinued). A favorite pen, with a brand-new ink cartridge. Small plastic cards with your name on them that can be used to purchase everything from gasoline to silk shirts to airplane tickets to Paris. Library cards, video club cards, photos of your niece and nephew, phone numbers, paint formulas, I can't go on. But you can see it all so clearly, you can almost touch it. As long as it's that clear, it's hard to believe it won't just come back at any moment. Then gradually, over days and weeks, it starts to fade. That's time, healing all wounds. That's letting go.

Sometimes something much more terrible than having your purse stolen happens—you hear an old friend from high school committed suicide, or they tell you your brother-in-law has AIDS—and you protect yourself psychically. You say it's terrible, it's terrible. You even cry a little. But somehow you don't let yourself really feel the full feeling. You don't let it get all the way in. It's too scary. Then something that is by contrast very minor will happen. Like the theft of the most beautiful purse in the world. And you just go for it. You wallow in it, you roll around in it, you poke it like a black-and-blue mark to see how bad it hurts. You walk around for days with a dark cloud over your head and yell at yourself and feel sorry for yourself and mourn. And think what a jerk you are, going completely nuts over a stupid purse, when your old high school friend is dead, your brother-in-law has AIDS, half the world is starving, and God knows what else.

So what I want to know is: who did it, and where is it now? I drive around my neighborhood, eyeing the little boys on their bikes and the sorority girls in their BMWs. I peek into other people's trash cans. I squint at their handbags. I peer into lighted windows at night. Was it you? I ask. No? Then who? Sometimes I think I'll get a phone call. Excuse me, the voice will say, are you Marion Winik? I think I've found something of yours. It gives me goose bumps just to imagine it.

The Landlady

became a landlady not by choice but by necessity. I had purchased a nice though small condominium at what seemed a reasonable price during a period that turned out to be the dizzy peak of a real estate market soon to collapse utterly. By the time the advent of small children forced me to seek more spacious and landed quarters, the place was worth half of what I had paid for it. I could not afford to sell, so I had to rent.

I expected to be good at it. My maternal grandfather, after all, made his living collecting rents in tenements in Harlem. I never met him, but I gather he was not an especially warm person. He was, on the other hand, a very effective property manager. I'm here for the rent, he would say, a chilly glint in his pale blue eyes. That was enough. The gun was to protect himself on the long trip downtown, his bulging leather case stuffed with cash.

The night I decided to rent the condo, I dreamed he was rapping on the door of what seemed to be my apartment. It was opened by a tall blond woman, and they fell into each other's arms.

Upon waking, I sat down with a mug of coffee and a thick white pad, the muse of classified advertising perched on my shoulder. TREETOP CONTEMPORARY, I scribbled. *Sunny 2-2 plus study, new carpet and tile, all appliances, microwave, W/D, vaulted ceilings with fans. Water paid. Call.*

Good for you! said the clerk when I phoned in my ad.

Just as I thought, I was born for this.

But if you don't mind my asking, she continued, is the tile saltillo? If it is, you should change the wording. People love saltillo. You know, I bet we can get this down to fifteen words so you can get our Friday to Sunday special.

Great, I said, and she slashed onward. All conjunctions must go.

The avalanche of calls I'm waiting for does not come. A few people want to know if the "study" might be used as an extra bedroom. Not really, I say, but it does have saltillo tile. One lady wants to move in with her husband and three children. We live in a trailer, she says. It will seem big to us.

There are college boys with loud voices who want a month-to-month lease and covered parking spaces. I picture them rubbing turtle wax into their BMWs while my microwave disappears under baked-on pizza splatter and my refrigerator is spray-painted with football slogans. Finally a professional-sounding woman asks me to describe the color scheme. Gray, I tell her. A very nice gray. It goes with anything. Then she mentions the baby grand piano.

I am visited by a rash of newly divorced men who have little furniture but lots of power tools and windsurfers. Where is the garage, they want to know. Unused to his awkward single state—there was still a faint difference in skin color where his wedding band had been—one curly-haired fellow blushed when I showed him the bedroom.

Before each showing, I spend frantic hours cleaning and straightening, polishing faucets, collecting baby toys. The closets are neat as a pin, but I can't seem to get anybody to look at them: once they realize I am the actual current inhabitant, they hurry through as if traversing an emergency room. They glance so quickly into the bathroom, they can't possibly have noticed the designer wallpaper.

This is a great complex, I tell them. Quiet, but friendly. I get the feeling I'm trying too hard.

One mildly interested fellow returns for a second look, accompanied by a trusted lady friend. There's a businesslike set to her features that doesn't bode well. She takes in the compact living-and-dining area with a single sweep of her shrewd little eyes. This is it? she asks him pointedly. I want to tell her about the track lighting, the low utility bills, the clever cabinet for storing trays and platters, but they are already gone.

Finally I can't take it anymore. We leave town for two weeks and turn the key over to a professional leasing agent. Half a month's rent seems a small price to pay.

By the time we return, a tall blond woman has leased our apartment. We move to a spacious rented house with a fenced yard, an eat-in kitchen, and most of the modern conveniences to which we grew so attached in the salad days of condominium life.

My blond lady calls to say that the clothes rod in the closet has come down, the electric outlet in the master bath doesn't work, and there's no place to keep her bike. Right, I feel like telling her; that's why I moved.

By the time I get there, she's dealt with the closet herself. A glimpse of her extensive wardrobe reveals the cause of the problem. Meanwhile, I switch off what I think is the breaker for the bathroom and get to work unscrewing the outlet plate. A half hour later, my efforts produce the desired result. Poking around inside to see if all the wires are connected, I notice a buzzing sensation in my fillings. I plug in a blow dryer; it roars into action. I fixed it, I announce calmly, as if this is something I do every day.

You could have been killed, she replies accusingly, as if thinking of the inconvenience it would have caused her.

I give her the chilly glint. Don't forget, rent's due on the first. Then I holster my screwdriver, shoulder my leather bag, and head home.

My grandfather the landlord was an energetic man who married three times before his death at fifty. His only surviving widow was a woman named Dot, a former Rockette and still a leggy sight for sore eyes when I met her. She and my mother had not been close during her tenure as stepparent and had completely lost touch after my grandfather's death. However, years later my mother ran into her at the counter at Schrafft's, and by that time we could use all the relatives we could get. Like some exiled tsarina, Dot was rehabilitated and returned to the family fold, where we all treated her with the mixture of fondness and obligation that is a grandmother's due.

Dot had a thousand pairs of gloves, a thousand pairs of shoes, a thousand scarves, a thousand rhinestone-encrusted barrettes. Her accessories were stored in every available nook and cranny of her midtown apartment, including the kitchen drawers and cabinets. She ate take-out Chinese food every day of her life, so had little use for cooking utensils. Her other prize possessions included a player piano and a small dog that had the face of a pit bull but was much more pleasant.

Dot loved to tell the story of how she met my grandfather, how he knocked at the door of her apartment on the day the rent was due. I'm here for the rent, he said gruffly, those blue eyes burning a hole in her heart. Dot could have fallen right into his arms. What most people saw as meanness, she took for a breathtaking manly quality. And he is gone but here she is in the same apartment after thirty-three years.

None of my tenants fall in love with me, and none stay for thirty-three years. The blond lady moves unexpectedly to Houston; the rental agent finds Bobby and Jason just in time for me to make my mortgage payment. Then Bobby and Jason also move to Houston, but it's just as well. You would think two big strong boys could deal with a thing like a running toilet. Next we get Esther, a godsend, a nice Jewish girl with a trust fund. She pays on time, she takes good care of the apartment, she installs a security system. She invites me to attend Kol Nidre services with her at the synagogue.

To my relief and delight, Esther renews her lease for a second year, but a few months into it, she calls to say she is planning an extended trip to South America. She wants to know if it is okay to sublet the apartment to a young woman she works with, Tricia. I know of her; I heard her interviewed on a local talk show. Just out of high school, she helps run an acclaimed environmental-awareness program. She's been staying with me here for a few months now, says Esther. She's a great girl. Amazing for her age.

The first few months go smoothly. In November, Tricia writes us a letter saying that the dryer broke. She had it fixed and is deducting $166.47 from the rent. I am happy I don't have to deal with it. Then in December, she doesn't pay at all. Doesn't even send Esther's check.

Throughout that month and the beginning of the next, I leave message after message on Tricia's (actually Esther's) machine. She occasionally calls back, usually at what is to her the end of a long night but is to me five o'clock in the morning. She is full of excuses and promises and calls me honey. I decide it is time to drop in unexpectedly and see what the hell is going on.

I arrive at the condo at midday; from the foot of the stairs, I can hear the music blasting behind the closed windows. "Souped up, cracked up, jacked up, smacked up, you're a bad scene and you need to be cleaned up," shouts some prescient English pop singer. If this is the sound track, I can't wait to see the movie.

The movie is a bunch of very stoned teenage girls sitting at the dining-room table smoking cigarettes and staring into space, among them Tricia. She is completely incoherent and her complexion is a mess. The table is surrounded by empty beer cans and other debris about a foot deep. In the living room, two sullen boys with expensive jackets and pagers sit by the phone.

*   *   *

Tricia calls me that night and confesses that she has fallen in with bad people. I can see that, but I've already phoned Esther's parents. They Fed Ex the rent I'm owed, and we call Esther in Ecuador. She wants to kick Tricia out, says she will come home to do it, but I convince her it isn't necessary. She's fallen in with bad people, I explain. But she's not malicious. I'll just tell her to get out.

And she does, leaving quite a mess behind her. Once we get the initial trash cleared out, it seems some things are missing. Where's Esther's bicycle? Tony asks. Wasn't there a TV on that table?

After we belatedly summon Esther back to Austin, we find out that not only did Tricia leave with the valuables and vandalize what she didn't take, but she also ran up Esther's credit cards, cleaned out her checking account, ignored the utility bills, paid her half of the rent with cash advances she got using Esther's ATM card, and did not have the dryer fixed after all. When the police retrieve Esther's Macintosh from a pawnshop, she finds a letter to J. Crew on the hard disk, written just two weeks after her departure. "Esther Greenberg gave me this pea green coat for Christmas two years ago," Tricia explains. "I've never worn it, and I hope it's not too late to exchange it for some new duds." In a P.S., she compliments the company for the excellent service she received from their telephone representative.

We also find a crumpled invitation to the Clinton inauguration and a journal that documents her childhood sexual abuse, her tortured lonely lustful teenage life, her downfall with drugs. There is not a word about the thefts, and the only mention of Esther is when Tricia writes that she fired the cleaning lady after the latter unfavorably compared their household habits.

Tricia has been arrested, is currently out on bail, and faces an impressive array of criminal and civil charges.

Esther is returning to the Galápagos, having spent three months putting her life back together and resurrecting her credit rating. Ironically enough, she too has been arrested, for unpaid tickets Tricia got while driving her car. She doubts she will ever be able to trust anyone again.

The gullible landlady is still at large. Despite all that has happened, she undoubtedly will trust again. She can't think why. Is it a curse, perhaps, placed long ago by some ruthlessly evicted Harlem mother of six on the descendants of the landlady's faithless grandfather?

The condominium itself is empty. The saltillo tile, bare of furniture, reflects the various gleamings of day and night through the slats of the miniblinds. The leasing agents escort prospective tenants through the silent rooms. It's perfect for you, they say. And the landlady's a dream.

Taking Hayes to Mexico

The *zapata* department of the Oaxaca *mercado* is hot and crowded, but I'm taking my time, checking out booth after booth of plastic sandals, slingbacks, spike heels, high tops, Mary Janes. Tony has my purse slung over one arm and fifteen-month-old Hayes in the other as I try on the cream-colored flats with the odd braided T-strap.

Emerging through a doorway into the open-air part of the market, I turn to make sure he's behind me. My eye is drawn instantly to my purse, hanging over Tony's shoulder. There is a long dark vertical slit in the woven fabric. Look at the purse, I say, my throat closing up. Just this morning I changed two hundred dollars' worth of traveler's checks.

But my wallet is still inside, stuffed in among the diapers, flip-flops, and tour books that protected it from the thief's searching fingers. Our hearts racing, we stumble on, to the woven bags and peppers and sweet breads and cakes, toys and Tupperware and white crumbly cheese, mangoes and squashes and rugs and urns and baskets big enough to live in. We can't spend that money fast enough.

When Hayes was born, I resolved to be the type of mother who takes her baby everywhere, who is seen dancing with him at parties, feeding him asparagus in restaurants, holding him up to the window on ferries and trains. I have pictures of his five-week-old bald head poking out of a hot tub in the Florida Keys; I remember being outraged because they wouldn't let me into a gay disco with him in the front-pack. He motored to New Orleans, camped in the Hill Country, went on business trips, and visited relatives. He seemed utterly unfazed by the unpredictable meals and beds of life on the road.

Nevertheless, people warned us that taking a toddler to Mexico might not be wise. A woman I met in the park one day knowingly advised, Don't take that blond baby down to Mexico! They'll get him for sure! She herself had just moved up from the Valley to protect her children from kidnapping by satanists.

Some of the warnings actually did come from sane and sober parents who spoke from experience. But I was not so easily discouraged.

In my younger days, I imagined myself somehow

exempt from mundane misfortune. Immune to germs, untouched by laws, riding through life on a magic carpet of propitious serendipity. If not, why didn't I get the flu when everyone else did? How come one time when I was doing a hundred miles per hour on the Garden State Parkway and got stopped by a policeman, he let me go? Fie, said I to those who saw danger and difficulty around every corner, and left my car windows rolled down when it looked like rain.

Over the years, life has presented me with plenty of evidence to unseat my delusions of invincibility. As big as a death, as small as a soaking-wet driver's seat. Then those benevolent dictators Pregnancy and Motherhood took over and really rearranged my furniture.

Still I manage to maintain a certain willful optimism, a knack for glossing over discouraging details. And look: every once in a while life throws a bone my way, like the thief in the market who didn't get away with my wallet.

At the friendly family-run guest house where we're staying in Oaxaca are several little boys whom Hayes adores. *El nene!* they call him. And his beach ball: *la pelota!* They toss the ball around the courtyard for hours, laughing and shrieking, Hayes toddling along behind them. He likes this much better than visiting ruins or shopping.

On the afternoon of the third day of our trip, *el nene* finally takes a decent nap. While he sleeps, I go down to the kitchen of the main house and bring back a plate of food for when he wakes up. I have him sitting naked in my lap on the bed, popping frijoles into his mouth, when we hear a distinct plop. And I thought the proprietress was overdoing it when she saw the baby and insisted on putting rubber sheets on our beds.

As we clean up, I notice that Hayes seems weak and a little warm to the touch. I ask Tony to run down the street to the health food place where we ate last night. It is managed by a sweet couple who have a daughter Hayes's age; maybe they know some mild herbal remedy.

By the time he returns, I've lost interest in mild herbal remedies. I don't need a thermometer to tell me Hayes is burning up. As fast as his fever rises, so do my guilt and panic. I try to think where I went wrong, and answers flood obediently to mind. What about the sad little girl in the square the other night who came up to our table during dinner, staring with hungry eyes at my plate of food? Without even thinking, I picked up my fork and gave her a bite. Didn't I give Hayes a bite off that same fork? What about that fleabag hotel room in Nuevo Laredo? What about the market and the street and the floor, Hayes picking up God knows what God knows where and putting it straight into his mouth?

Into the main house I fly, begging someone to call a doctor. The grandmother phones their family physician while I collapse on a divan, hugging Hayes to my chest. Remedies are offered from all sides: the herbal formula, half an aspirin dissolved in boiled water, a medication

Concepción tells me cured the night fevers of each of her children. I go back to my room to wait for the doctor. Outside the night is dark but in the room the light is yellow, and I sit in the rocking chair with Hayes, staring straight ahead.

Word of our trouble spreads quickly through the guest house. An American woman stops by, offering alfalfa-mint tea. I tell her the doctor is on his way. Watch out, she says. Their solution for everything is a shot of penicillin. Moments later, young Doctor Hermán Tenorio Vasconcelos arrives. His gentle, competent demeanor and almost perfect English are very soothing. He diagnoses "big red tonsils" and prescribes, guess what, penicillin. And suppositories to bring down the fever.

Shots? Suppositories? This kid has barely had two drops of children's Tylenol in his life. But Dr. Hermán insists. Maybe if you were at home, he says, you could just watch him for a few days. Here, you must give the antibiotic right away. Do you know how to shot?

Do we know how to shot? I look at Tony, who knew me in the good old days of IV drug abuse, when I carried a ten-pack of hypodermic syringes in my coat pocket. But I was never very good at the actual procedure, and I certainly don't feel up to it now.

Oh sure, he tells the doctor bravely, I can do it, and they speed off to the *farmacia*.

Soon after he takes the medication, Hayes falls

asleep. I wish I had a shrine to the Virgin so I could put this bottle of penicillin on it.

In the morning, *milagro* of *milagros*, Hayes is chasing ducks and kittens as if nothing ever happened. We rinse out a large pile of bedsheets and baby clothes and hang them to dry on the roof. Then we are suddenly starving. Breakfast is magenta watermelon and sunny pineapple, *flautas*, *chilaquiles*, eggs with *salsa verde*.

Travel does have its discomforts, though they are usually outweighed by its pleasures, at least if you are old enough to know what you are doing and why. An uncomfortable bus ride, a bad meal, an unfriendly tour guide: you can handle it, because it's all part of the adventure. On the other hand, if you are so young that you have no sense of place at all, it makes no difference whether you are traveling or not. You sleep on the bus, spit out the food, don't even know the tour guide exists.

Hayes is at a tricky age between these two states. He is certainly aware that he's not at home, that life is not going on as usual. The absence of certain key items— his crib, his kitchen floor—does not escape him. Once a predictable domestic sitcom, his life has suddenly become a fast-paced *National Geographic* documentary, complete with exotic locales and a cast of thousands.

Most of the time, he throws himself into the action with enthusiasm and is received the same way. When it occasionally becomes a bit overwhelming, he claims my body as his all-purpose home away from home. His food source, his chaise longue, his camel, his human security blanket. When he's in that mood, I just tie him on my hip with a woven Oaxacan shawl, positioning him with his mouth directly in line for *la leche*. Chi-chi, they call it down here. Baby wants cheech.

In Puerto Angel, we stay at a beautiful *posada* hidden in a shady canyon, with pure water from a spring, delicious vegetarian food, interesting fellow guests on the patio.

Hayes has recovered from his fever and is ready for the beach. For three days, the red shovel never leaves his hand. I come back to the *palapa* with sodas and find him and his father snoozing side by side in a hammock. He picks up a special shell, carries it around for hours, then drops it to embrace a skinny beach dog. Woof, he says, fluent in international dog language.

Unfortunately, whatever has gone awry with Hayes's digestive system has not gone away. Turista in third-world disposable diapers—I'll say no more.

During our stay at the beach I notice that I alternate between being wildly nervous about every single thing Hayes does—Get that knife away from him! Look, he's heading for the edge! That sand is too hot! What did he just put in his mouth?—and then getting wrapped up in my book for half an hour and not looking up at all. Then I catch myself and snap to attention.

The American woman who runs our *posada* tells me that in this part of Mexico, people don't even take their babies out of the house, to make sure no one will give them the evil eye. If they must go out, they are swaddled in blankets right up to their heads.

I don't want to know this.

The morning we head up the coast to Puerto Escondido, Hayes has a relapse. Diarrhea raging, he is listless and sweaty. We plan to stay at the Hotel Santa Fe, a place with air-conditioned rooms and a swimming pool, where we can make him a bit more comfortable, we hope.

We arrive at the Santa Fe in the unblinking heat of noon and are told we must wait an hour for a room to be ready. We are in despair. Our son is very ill, we plead.

Oh yes, we had another baby here once with thees same thing, the reception clerk tells us.

Really, says Tony, what happened?

He dead, she says.

A cab takes us downtown to the *médico*, but he's out for siesta. We buy some popsicles and sit down on the curb to wait. At first I am overjoyed to see how much Hayes is enjoying the lime ice. Then I realize it's made of water.

We've got to get out of here. Though we're scheduled to spend two more days in Escondido, I think we've had all the fun that's coming our way. Tony goes off to find a travel agent and get us on the first flight out in the morning.

Meanwhile Doctor Zósimo Silva Luna strolls up, dressed in white polyester. No Doctor Hermán, this guy is an undistinguished schmo who sits in his dismal office across the street from the tourist strip, writing scripts for gringos with swimmer's ear and Montezuma's revenge. After listening impassively to my description of Hayes's symptoms, he prescribes more shots of penicillin. Penicillin? For diarrhea? Yes, he says. Stupid with desperation, I give in.

Walking back, we see a mural on the turquoise wall of an exterminator's office: the hobo mouse, dreaming of death, ties up his cheese in a red bandanna and gets out of town.

The next morning before we leave, I go to the bank to get a cash advance with my Visa card. Having held up admirably until now, standing in line I am suddenly gripped by panic. A slide show of horrifying images begins in my head. Hayes lying motionless, skin pale, eyes closed. Hospitals, gurneys, ambulances. Tony running across the street, coming to give me dreadful news. Where's my baby? I bolt from the line and rush back to the hotel.

Everything is just as I left it: Tony is packing; Hayes is weakly chewing on a saltine. We are on our way home.

By the time we land in Nuevo Laredo, we have run out of diapers. I spot a lady with a baby and ask her if she has an extra. She hands me a Pampers. An American one! Seeing my joy, she forces me to take a few more. I fondle them lovingly.

I pick up Hayes, Tony shoulders the luggage, and we head out to look for a cab. But when I reach the curb, he's not behind me. Puzzled, I reenter the terminal. I don't see him anywhere. It is a sign of my state of mind at this point that I actually believe he's been nabbed by satanists.

As soon as we get back into Texas, I go straight to a pay phone to call my pediatrician. She doesn't seem too worried. Gatorade, she says, not penicillin.

Within forty-eight hours, Hayes is fine. We're never quite sure whether the stomach thing was related to the throat thing, or if he did have a case of turista, and then, to complicate matters further, we find out that several of his baby friends were sick the week we were gone, some with diarrhea. I'm embarrassed by how relieved I am to hear this.

In the photographs, everything is perfect. Hayes in the courtyard with Alfredo and the beach ball. Hayes counting beans in the *mercado*. Riding a merry-go-round near the ruins at Mitla. Half-covered with sand at the water's edge, watching a wild mustang gallop by.

When people ask about our trip to Mexico, we never know quite what to say. There's the Good Trip and the Bad Trip, each impossible to remember or talk about without the other jumping up to interrupt. No, we didn't exactly prove the skeptics wrong, but we're not about to say we've learned our lesson.

It's like the monkey-bear, a pull toy we bought Hayes in the market at Oaxaca. An absurd blue plastic bear's head on the body of a furry brown-and-orange monkey, it pedals a handmade tin tricycle when you pull the string. Crazily conceived but bravely executed nonetheless, it's a mistake that on second look becomes a treasure.

Off the Road, and On

Though I am She Who Hates to Drive, Stop Sign–
Running Girl, the notorious Lady Get the Hell off
the Road, though automobile makes and models
don't mean a thing to me, in my own obscure female
way, I love cars. I love what happens inside them. Not
pistons and camshafts; not driving per se, at least not
the tedious track from house to office to school to store
and home again. I just can't seem to sustain the state of
patient, cautious attention required to avert missed turns
and moving violations, vulgar gestures and violent emotions, jagged bits of orange taillight lens in the driveway. On the way home from work, I have to make this
hard right curve past a cemetery, and sometimes I think
I might as well just get it over with.

What I love is not maneuvering the car but just
spending time in it, eating, talking, kissing, sleeping,

smoking. Some would rather be fishing; I would rather be parked in the car by the lake. The privacy and intimacy of the automobile, the low-roofed, front-facing, body-hugging, many-windowed carchitechture, narrow the focus and intensify the emotional tone of everything that transpires inside.

I've always felt this way. If we couldn't persuade our parents to take us to Stewart's Drive-in Root Beer, my sister and I would pack up a sack of sandwiches and beat a trail to my mother's Le Mans in the driveway. We much preferred the seclusion and comfort of the blue leatherette interior to the dubious advantages of a more rustic setting. We adjusted the rearview mirrors to monitor activity in the street behind us (Look, Daniel Malachowsky just fell off his bike!) and rolled down the window just enough to accommodate the antenna of a transistor radio. Long after the food was gone, we'd be in there with our feet up on the dash, listening to "Build Me Up, Buttercup" as often as the deejay would play it.

Though after puberty, eating was no longer my favorite parked-car activity, years later I would rejoice at a blown-out tire on the way to a Labor Day picnic and convince three friends to spend the afternoon drinking beer and passing deviled eggs in a broken-down yellow convertible by the side of the road. Funny how sometimes the good life has to sneak up and catch you from behind.

Missing the drive-in-movie era did not prevent me from discovering that there is no better place for oral sex than the front seat of a car. From the moment your fingers slip from the key in the ignition and you twist toward him, lips touching over the stick shift, bodies drawing together like magnets against the relentless forward orientation of the bucket seats, your passion is amplified. It quickly expands to fill the space, reflects back on itself, condenses on the glass. You climb across and kneel in his lap, bending to kiss his upturned face, his half-closed eyes. His fingers weave through your hair, tightening and pulling hard. Headlights catch the white lace of your bra, tossed onto the swell of the back seat as you slide down to the floorboards, but nothing can stop you now. No matter what your age, you are in the great tradition of teenage sluts as you fit your body beneath the glove compartment and unbutton his jeans.

Whether parked or in motion, the car is also ideal for the less racy but potentially no less intimate act of conversation. Like the cone of silence lowered by secret agents and heads of state in television sitcoms, the glass-and-metal cocoon is conducive to the confiding of secrets, to gossip, analysis, confession, complaint, romantic petition. It is one of the few conversational venues in which there is no awkwardness about where to look when you don't want to meet the other person's eyes. If it doesn't go well, you can drive home, lay your head down on the steering wheel, and cry. And should you fall asleep, perhaps some kindly person bigger than you will come and lift you out and carry you to bed.

The ultimate car experience, combining the potential of all others, is the long-distance road trip. While it does involve driving, even Stop Sign–Running Girl can hold the wheel straight and press the gas pedal. On in-town excursions, every place between the starting point and the destination is a mere annoyance. But on interstate voyages, you pass through not geography but poetry, through place-names themselves, brand-new, promising, crisp white on green. Big Spring. Red Rocks. Bound Brook. You are not in these towns. You are in the car.

You don't just use it, you become one with it. The metal rim of the window is warm in the crook of your arm as your hand dangles outside, surfing the wind. You find you can drive with your foot, either one, left or right. And if you go too fast, it's not because you're in a hurry but because you like to. You and your car, you eat miles for lunch. Cops for dinner. Speeding tickets for breakfast.

At the start of the trip, you and your companion have a million things to talk about. All are dispatched in the first three hours, then you are cranky for another three, then that too passes and you are quiet. The wind in the roof rack becomes the sound of your thoughts. You wait and wait for Nashville, then are there and it makes no difference, except afterward the signs say how far to Memphis.

You invent grown-up car games. If you could go back to school and major in anything, what would it be? Architecture?!? Really? Some days I think pure mathematics. Or maybe I'd do history again but remember it this time. When we get home let's have a dinner party. Who should we have? What should we eat? I'll make a list. If you could sleep with any movie star, living or dead, who would it be? Want me to read to you? *People, National Enquirer*, or *The Sound and the Fury*?

Tuscaloosa. Should we stop here? How much gas do we have left? Every fill-up, each meal, every bathroom break, is the subject of elaborate deliberation. It makes you feel as if you're getting somewhere, if only somewhere to pee. As if you have something to look forward to, if only French fries and a can of soda. You thrive on this elevation of mundane necessities into special events, throw yourself into interpreting maps and billboards.

At last, you fall out of the car weak as rag dolls, charging sodas and chips and cigarettes and gum along with the gas so your mouths will be busy every minute. You've been driving so long that when you switch seats you can't change perspective and keep ducking the trucks that look as if they're coming right at you from the frontage road. You keep your eye on the odometer, constantly recalculating percent completion and average miles per hour, infuriated when the miles-to-go signs don't agree with your numbers. If Shreveport was one hundred forty miles away twenty miles ago, how the hell can it be one hundred twenty-three miles away now?

Don't even think about the shortest distance between two points. You've fallen for that one a million times

before. Gotten off the highway to avoid a ninety-degree
angle, driven some teeny hypotenuse road through every
backwoods cow pasture small town traffic light speed
trap in the U.S.A. Sometimes it's beautiful, yes. Often
there is better food. But it is never shorter. Myself, I've
even believed there was a road because there should be
a road, because you shouldn't have to go all the way
back up through the mountains to Guadalajara to get to
Acapulco; and when there was no road, I drove my
trusty red wagon through jungles and rivers. What I
learned: *desviación* means "detour" in Spanish. *Obsti-
nado* means "stubborn."

No matter how things are in real life, you get in the
car and there is nothing for you but going on. You've
already missed your turnoff, mistaken the landmarks,
forgotten your intentions; you might as well go ahead
and get out of town. Drive until sunset ignites the white
lines that connect you to the horizon. Until dark, when
possibility blooms beneath the asphalt and the air from
the dashboard vents is cold and clean. Until morning,
when you stop and settle down, rent a little house by the
highway, and watch the cars go by. Like Jack Kerouac
and all the rest of them, get out of the car and imagine
there is something left to say.

Domestic Arrangements

see a couple with a tiny baby at a party; they are so happy. I go over to *ooh* and *aah* at the baby and ask to hold him. I have two boys, I say.

Oh, really? How old?

Two and four.

Is that hard?

It's hell.

They exchange looks. Is this a depraved person to whom they are speaking, or is it the voice of doom resonating from their future?

When I see this in their faces, I start rambling, trying to explain. Well, it's so awful, really, I begin. They never listen to me, never, and I turn into a maniac. I scream, sometimes I spank them, which I thought I would never do, but they won't listen any other way. I never realized how demanding it would be, how much it would compete with other things in my life. When I'm working, I feel bad about not being with them. When I'm with them, I ignore them half the time, turn on the TV, or send them outside and go do something else. No matter what I do, I feel guilty. And it's hard on your marriage. They fight all the time, the big one is mean to the little one, maybe it's their ages, I don't know. I'm sure it will get better. Though people with teenagers tell me it's the most intense of all. You guys enjoy this time. Having one little infant is dreamland. It's never the same again. Unless he has colic or something.

They are staring with thinly disguised horror. Don't get me wrong, I assure them. I love my kids. I wouldn't trade them for anything. If I had it to do over, I would.

It's too late, however, to convince them I have any maternal instincts or redeeming qualities. As I hand them their baby back they smile politely and make a beeline for the other side of the room. It could be contagious.

I did not get into the business of Marriage and Children, Inc., without big ideas about how homes should be run and how kids should be raised. Interweaving feminist theories with conclusions based on personal experience, I formed my ideal of how the egalitarian, emotionally healthy, politically correct postnuclear family could operate.

Children should be raised by their parents, not by

paid help or preschools, I thought. Men and women should divide household and parenting duties equally and not necessarily along traditional gender lines. This would be easy, I assumed, because once you are a parent, you are magically filled with all the qualities it takes to raise kids, like patience, energy, and wisdom. It is odd that people think this, even in the innocence of childlessness, since God knows nobody thinks their own parents did it right, and then there's the recurrent nightmare of the daily news.

An article in *The New York Times* about mothers in prison discussed whether they should be allowed to keep their babies. In a survey, they asked these women—whose own childhoods had invariably been rough—if they thought they would be better mothers than their own mothers had been. They didn't. I was not as surprised at this as the author was.

How do you judge your mother and say she was bad and you're going to be better? She wasn't perfect, but neither are you. The fact that she loved you as best she could has had to be good enough. You want it to be good enough for your own children.

At the same time, you don't want to make exactly the same mistakes they did, the ones you've been bitching about to therapists all these years. One of my own enlightened precepts, the idea that I should raise my children at home without paid help, is typical of a parenting ideal formed in reaction to one's own childhood.

My father was a textbook-case workaholic, gone from

seven in the morning till at least seven-thirty at night, when we'd race through the house as if the mechanical thunder of the garage door heralded the Second Coming. After dinner, he'd sit right down at his adding machine, or later his PC, in front of the TV. Weekends, more of the same. It just figures that he died while we were in our twenties, heart attack, of course, and certainly didn't spend any time with us after that.

My mother was around a lot more than my father, but she was also very busy. She played golf, bridge, and tennis, did a little work for my father's company, talked on the phone, organized their busy social life. On the other hand, she was class mother year after year, drove an ungodly number of carpools, and orchestrated the endless excessive birthday parties of our dreams. But parents do not seem to get time off for good behavior.

The history of my childhood was divided into reigns, like those of Catherine the Great and Ivan the Terrible, except that our occasionally benign despot was chosen not by bloodline or birthright but according to the difficulties of finding and keeping live-in domestic employees. The first in the dynasty was a German nanny whom I know only through a sixteen-millimeter black-and-white home movie of my mother leaving Mt. Sinai Hospital after I was born. The car pulls up, my mother appears, smiling and waving, and I am bringing up the rear, swaddled and carried by the nanny. Look, my mother says whenever we watch the film. There's Trudy.

We moved from New York to New Jersey when I was

two, the year Nancy was born. Trudy did not come with us. Instead we were taken care of by a series of black live-in maids, for whom our house was, in general, a layover between the place they were escaping from and the place they hoped to end up. Mainly it was girls from the islands, whom my mother sponsored for U.S. work permits, and girls from the South on their way to the big city. Our family cuisine swung wildly between Caribbean pork chops and Southern fried chicken.

There was Johnnie Mae, Jeannie Mae, Ella Mae. Dolly, Dory, and Daphne. My sister and I generally referred to them by their preferred mode of punishment. The Pincher, for example.

There was a typed list of duties for the maid, which I pored over: Monday, living room and bathrooms; Tuesday, laundry and bedrooms; every other Wednesday off. This list defined some mystery for me. I remember begging to be assigned chores, like the kids in *Cheaper by the Dozen*. Looking back, I realize that the maid's most important duty was not even on the list. Us. We were every day.

My sister and I shared a room, and the maid of the moment slept next door, in a room with red carpet and a fold-out sofa bed with a leopard corduroy slipcover. It was in that room that I watched JFK's funeral on television, with Nancy and Johnnie Mae crying. It was in that room that I learned to dance the Funky Chicken and listened over and over to a song called "Mashed-Potato Time."

Recently I got a little drunk and had this horribly embarrassing conversation with a young black woman I know, a gorgeous dreadlocked lesbian who was featured on the cover of a national magazine as one of the country's leading campus activists. It was a Mammy thing, how I was raised by black people and have this childhood connection to black culture, how I'm always trying to get back to it. Like if I am at a fancy nightclub that has an attendant in the ladies' room, I usually end up spending the evening in there with her, straightening up the hairbrushes and talking about God knows what. My activist friend did not seem very moved by my plight.

My initial plan as a mother was, naturally, to do it all myself. For one whole year after Hayes was born, I would not leave him with a babysitter. Not only was I nursing, but I carried with me the childhood resolve that I would never do to my own children this terrible thing that was done to me.

The night we finally left him with a sitter, we went to a restaurant just a couple of blocks from the house. I called midway through dinner and heard Hayes shrieking in the background. I flew out the door and ran all the way home in high heels. After paying the babysitter and sending her off, I took Hayes back to the restaurant for dessert. Soon after, I refused to attend a cousin's wedding because no children, not even babies, were allowed.

As Hayes got older and could not so easily be taken to adult gatherings, my attitude began to change. He'd be better off at home, I thought, with his toys and his movies and his own bed. But does this mean that I should deprive myself of grown-up fun? I thought not. Then my second son was born, and it became an even bigger pain in the ass to take them places where there was nothing for them to do and lots of things for them to break, to restaurants or parties or shows for which their attention span was a tenth of my own. Now, I must confess, I have a babysitter about one evening a week. If I get invited to some adults-only event, it's a red-letter day.

One night a week off from small children doesn't seem like much to ask. I try to remember: Is this how much my parents went out, really, and did it just seem like all the time? Will it seem like that to my children?

I used to think of the fact that I started school at two as further evidence of my parents' lack of interest. They couldn't wait to get me out of the house! However, when Hayes attained the age of two, I began to notice how much he loved to play with other little kids. I could see how he enjoyed singing and duck-duck-goose and making necklaces out of painted macaroni. When I didn't have the energy to orchestrate these activities, he quickly became bored and difficult. What to do? Montessori, of course, which he adored. So on this bum rap as well, my convicted parents must be pardoned.

Though I don't yearn for live-in help at the moment,

I've learned never to say never. When Tony went away for two weeks last summer, I hired a young woman to help me with the boys. Mostly she watched them while I was at the office, Tony's usual tour of duty, but a few days I stayed home to write and had her come in anyway. It pains me slightly to admit that I loved it. I loved being able to have lunch with them or play with them for an hour and then say, Meredith, could you come get the kids, I need to get back to work, and not feel that I was imposing or using up favors or not doing my job. Which takes us to the ongoing drama of dividing domestic chores with one's spouse.

As do most women of my generation, I believe that men should be involved fifty-fifty around the house. Unlike many gals, however, I managed to get a husband who actually does his share. You never know what evil lurks behind the liberated linc and the ponytail; you marry them and take them home and they forget they ever saw a can of Comet. With a husband who does laundry and mops floors in addition to dealing with manly challenges such as lawn-mowing, I can hardly complain.

But redefining gender roles in the domestic arena is a tricky thing; the division of labor can be loaded with tension. Everything I do around the house I seem to think I'm doing "for" Tony. When I wash the dishes or make the beds, all the little everyday stuff, I feel I deserve some kind of recognition, some Brownie points. Everything he does he thinks of in terms of money. How much would I, the main breadwinner, have to pay to get this job done if he were not there to do it? It's so exhausting and so stupid. Sometimes I wonder if we aren't just reversing the traditional male-female attitudes. I fantasize about living in a commune or on a kibbutz, where the work is split among a greater number of adults and, at least in my imagination, they don't hate one another over it.

On some days, even parenting falls into the realm of tedious trade-off: one takes the kids to the park for a while, or stays home so the other can go out, and the free one is grateful, and guilty, already thinking about the payback. The grunt-work of raising children is more challenging than keeping house, and sharing it is an even bigger deal.

Ever since I read Nancy Chodorow in college, I've been convinced that sexism can be ended only by a generation of boys and girls who are equally nurtured by both parents, who see parents of both genders changing diapers and pouring apple juice and sitting on the bench at the playground, working and leaving and coming back. The idea is that when children form their concepts of themselves and of the opposite sex in this environment, the psychological foundation of sexism will no longer exist.

In perhaps this one regard alone, my adult life conforms to my youthful ideals. At our house, the daddy switched to part-time work after one child was born, and moved his hair salon to the house after the second. My

boys are growing up with a father who's around almost
all the time, who not only works for money but changes
beds, packs lunches, and applies Band-Aids. Though
this means a great deal to me, I am no longer sure it will
change the world; I don't even know how it weighs in
against the male stereotypes they get from TV and stories and other people. Maybe they'll end up following in
the footsteps of their neurotic mother, forever trying to
bond with kindly janitors who remind them of Daddy.

The relationship between how people are brought up
and how they turn out cannot be reduced to any simple
formula. In the face of this—like the mothers in prison,
like your own mother, like everybody else you know—
you do what you think is right. And when you can't
always live up to that, you do the best you can.

Here's how tired I am sometimes. En route from the
office to the kids' school, already late, I pull up at a red
light behind a car with a bumper sticker that reads *Don't
Postpone Joy*. I stare blankly for a moment. Running on
just enough stress to catapult me past exhaustion, I
can't imagine having the time or energy to entertain joy,
should it unexpectedly arrive.

Averting my eyes from the bumper sticker, I notice
a sign outside a hamburger joint across the street. WEL-
COM MUSIC FESTIVAL PARTICIPANT! This is the last straw; I
almost burst into tears. At this moment, these four words
somehow represent the very essence of hope and hard

work, entrepreneurship and enthusiasm. The people who conceived the music festival, organized it, and publicized it; the musicians who will play at it and the people who have traveled to hear them; the reporters and shopkeepers and restaurant owners all trying to make their respective hay; the kid who climbed the ladder to put up the red marquee letters. The sheer presence of all this energy swirling around me is overwhelming, completely enervating.

Yet if I can make it through the rest of the day—if I can have a peaceful afternoon with the kids and if they eat their dinner and hear their stories and go to bed on time, if they do not whine and fight and break things, if I do not lose my temper, if Hayes does not cheat at checkers, if Tony is in a decent mood—it will, in fact, be joy. And I will not postpone it.

Some of My Best Friends

Recently a friend of mine speculated that if he weren't gay, he would wish to be, because it's so much cooler than being straight. Disco, deco, gossip columns, movie musicals, haute couture, miniature dog breeds, fifties furniture—without gay men, he asked, would any of these cultural phenomena exist or be properly appreciated? Not that gay sensibility is limited to camp and kitsch. Another gay hero of mine is a mountain climber, a Trotskyist theoretician, a lover of classical music, fine painting, and small, dark Italian chocolates with gooey centers.

Straight women like me have cherished the friendship of gay men since Mona posed for Leonardo, since Antony helped Cleopatra redo the palace. With our sympathetic, easy-to-talk-to gay male friends, we women are free to be ourselves. Turn off the sexual tension, and we're suddenly sane. At least until we fall in love with them; then we go nuts again.

Admittedly, there are gay men who don't like women and can be rather nasty about it. Some simply pretend that we don't exist; others are more virulent. A, one of our leading American poets despite the fact that most people can't make heads or tails of his work, is the first example that comes to mind. At one point in my academic career I was enrolled in a poetry tutorial with A, as part of a creative writing program that I had entered largely because he was the head of it.

But A was uninterested in me or my work, or in the work of the other women writers in the program. The dashing young male graduate students, on the other hand, showed great potential. Already having an A-esque tone in their work (this was not an official requirement for getting into the program, but it certainly didn't hurt), they soon became full-fledged clones.

When it was time to schedule my tutorial, A and I discovered that we lived in the same building. Since the campus was a major trek across town, we decided to meet every other week at his apartment. I was quite nervous that first Tuesday, riding the elevator up to the Great Man's living room at 10:30 A.M.

I had to press the buzzer so many times I began to think I had the wrong place. As I was about to give up, the door was opened by a mustachioed young man in a terry-cloth robe. He'll be with you in a moment, he said, not quite inviting me in. I stood in the doorway for about ten minutes, listening to water running, doors opening and closing, and muffled voices.

At last A appeared. We sat on the couch and he began to look over the work I had submitted. He seemed hard-pressed to think of anything to say about it, and finally began to critique a fanciful little poem on the subject of doing the dishes on the basis that it was not realistic, not an accurate, literal description of the dish-washing process. I found this somewhat hard to take, coming from a man whose own writing was completely divorced from real life and causal logic as we know it. I concluded then and there that A, like the other great faggot-poet of my acquaintance, G, was your basic misogynist ingrate.

Some gay men don't like us; well, we don't like them either. But it's worth noting that there are plenty of straight men who don't like women, often with more devastating results. Better a gay misogynist than a straight rapist or wife-beater. Maybe some of these so-called straight guys should *become* gay misogynists.

Lesbians, on the other hand, love women. This I find perfectly charming.

Sometimes I wish I were gay myself, so I could be militant about it. There is no better way to show that you think there's nothing wrong with homosexuality than to be gay and not try to hide it. I would just love to come out to my relatives, neighbors, and co-workers, to market researchers and census takers, to real estate agents and policemen, to anyone who happened to ask or notice. Of course, that's easy for me to say; as a straight person, there are things I just don't understand, nasty little truths I've never had to learn.

Last spring, it took three lesbian friends to hold me down and explain that we really shouldn't dance with each other in a country-western kicker bar in South Texas. To me, it was all in fun, there weren't enough guys to dance with anyway, and hey, whaddya say, *épater les bourgeois*! To Liz, Margaret, and Jen, it was asking for trouble. They had seen it before: how a room can change, how a friendly bartender turns terse and rude, how a happy, beery, partner-swingin' crowd becomes something else.

It makes me mad that my gay friends have to live in this gay-hating and -fearing culture, have to have it rub off on them. That they have to hear voices that say they're perverted and weird, that what makes them feel good is sick, that they don't deserve love and happiness, that they do, indeed, have something shameful to hide.

For God's sake, what? Homosexuality is a natural and common form of human behavior. I can't understand what's supposed to be so crazed about it. Just that it doesn't produce offspring? A lot of the things straight people do in bed don't produce offspring either. We rarely even have intercourse without devices designed to thwart its natural outcome. If any sexual act that doesn't make babies is perverted, we're all in big trouble.

Even in the animal kingdom, not everyone is straight. I read that there are lesbian seagulls living on an island off the coast of California. As the former owner of a gay dog, I am not surprised by this. Ali Baba Bumbala Rasa Compala Zaza LeHaza, or Ali, as he was more often called, was never much interested in female dogs to begin with. They don't call them bitch for nothing, he was heard to growl. Then during his first and last attempt at straight sex, which occurred in a parking lot on a college campus, he got stuck in the penetration pose for over an hour and had to be hosed down with cold water, in plain view of gawking and greatly amused passersby.

That was the end of that. He joined up with a pack of boisterously masculine, fun-loving dogs, who had normal names and sweet, simple natures. Though he clearly lusted after the golden retriever and the shepherd-pinscher mix, neither returned his interest. He became increasingly depressed and finally ran away from home. I can only hope he found his niche in dog society—perhaps the canine equivalent of that California island, or possibly Key West.

In any case, to equate human relationships with the social behavior of other species is to sadly reduce all affairs of the heart. Neither seagulls nor dogs make valentines or have long-distance romances or compose symphonies for their beloveds. Even in heterosexual relationships, there is something more at work than simple biological imperatives. Like psychology, for instance. From a Freudian perspective, heterosexual love is founded on the desire to possess the mysterious Other. But homosexuality does not rely on this. By making members of one's own sex the object of desire, homosexual love affirms the lovability of the self. Maybe that's what's so abnormal about it.

My first lesbian friend, back in my early twenties, was an older woman named Sky. Our friendship was only slightly complicated by her stronger feelings for me. While putting up with my impassioned flings with cold cowboys and troubled teenagers, she introduced me to the staples of seventies lesbian life: Holly Near, Teresa Trull, Cris Williamson, and the other founding mothers of lesbo-folk, Tarot cards, herbal tea, feminist psychology, the timeless institution of the dyke bar. I was dazzled; in some ways, all I wanted was to be part of it.

But as both gay and straight people know, one's sexuality is not something one chooses, like a major in college, or changes at will, like a hair color. My apparently hopeless hetero-ness doesn't stop me from respecting gay people in general, from admiring and enjoying gay culture, or from loving a great many gay people individually. As far as I'm concerned, no consensual sex act is ever the business of anyone but the partners involved (and, of course, the close friends with whom they choose to gossip about it afterward). On the other hand, building a society where all forms of love are respected and where private prejudices don't make public policy is everybody's business.

We are all supposedly entitled to life, liberty, and the pursuit of happiness. Many gay people now have one out of three, if they're lucky. We can do better than that.

Visiting Steven

am walking through Greenwich Village with Steven
again, past the snooty cafés and the democratic delis,
the sidewalk montage of shoes and coats and hairdos
and shopping bags. We talked about seeing a movie,
about taking the train uptown, but in the end we just put
on our coats and walked out the door. We talk and we
walk and he smokes, and if he gets mad or upset he
walks a little faster and I lag a few steps behind, following the familiar beat-up leather jacket with the
sweatshirt hood sticking out of the collar. Now he waits
for me to catch up, exhales a drag of the cigarette.
Wanna stop for coffee? he says, in that North Jersey
tough-guy gravel voice.

We have a lot of things to talk about, none of them
easy, and I am in the city for only a couple of days. After
a thirteen-year relationship that began when they were

still teenagers, my sister, Nancy, left Steven a few years ago. She had her reasons. I've come to accept them. He hasn't. We haven't seen each other much since then, and now we're together for the first time not as part of a threesome or foursome; it's just us. If we're going to be friends now, it's only because we like each other. But somehow, neither of us can leave the past behind: he can't let go of the hurt and I can't stop trying to explain, wanting him to forgive her.

We talk about this so much and are both so passionate and angry, drinking our coffee, eating our omelettes, walking down the street again, buying sunglasses from a Rastafarian, walking some more, that it might almost seem to be the reason for my visit. I wish it were. But I am here because Steven is sick. He has AIDS.

What has it been—six years?—since the positive HIV test? And until recently it didn't slow him down at all. As he had since high school, he worked as a carpenter, remodeling apartments, building bookshelves for law offices. In his spare time, he had his painting: suicides and triangles on canvas by day, pastel T-shirt graffiti slapped on brick walls in the middle of the night. He took acting classes. He and Nancy traveled to Thailand, India, Italy, Portugal. Unfortunately, in the midst of this they also did way too many drugs, and by the time they stopped, he had HIV, she didn't, and they didn't have much of a marriage left. Soon after the breakup, the HIV moved from the background to the foreground.

In the past year, Steven's had a bout of AIDS-related pneumonia, a rare disease of the optic nerve, and some mysterious ailment he described as a "fungus in my brain." Sometime around Christmas he stopped going to work. Come down and stay here with us for a while, I kept saying on the phone, standing by the kitchen window of my home in Texas. We'll sit by the pool. We'll eat Mexican food. It'll be good for you.

Yes, he would say, I want to come.

As the months went by, I realized I was being unrealistic. He was on intravenous medicine for the eye problem, was seeing doctors several times a week, and sometimes did not have the energy to leave his apartment.

Then one afternoon I was sitting on a friend's porch, talking to a visitor from New York who also knew Steven. At first, we discussed his illness, but gradually I found myself telling her about the early days of our friendship. The summer afternoon in '77 when Nancy and Sandye and I met Steven and his friend Mark at a swimming pool here in Austin, a bunch of born-to-run New Jersey kids who recognized one another by their accents and the bag of bagels. How they and their dogs moved into the place we were sharing with two other girls, and we all paid thirty bucks a month rent until we got thrown out for having six people and four pets in a two-bedroom house. How Steven and I went out on a date before he and Nancy ever got together; how we argued the whole night and basically have been arguing ever since.

It doesn't matter if they've split up, I said, about to cry. I'm still his sister. That was the day I decided to go to New York.

Until the minute I left, I had doubts about the trip. I didn't know whether I'd be seeing him on a good weekend or bad, whether I'd be sitting by his hospital bed or at his kitchen table. Either way, I was nervous about what he would look like, what toll the illness had taken on the strong, compact body and the handsome Italian features. And, I worried, does the fact that I'm going mean he really is dying? And if so—grimly practical now—should I wait until later? How many trips like this can I afford? Or deal with?

Finally, as I moved through an airport full of business travelers and vacationers, I let my anxiety become anticipation. I hadn't seen Steven in a year; I missed him. It felt right to go to his side. We are connected, I thought; this is what being connected means. I slung my carry-on bag over my shoulder and boarded the plane.

The taxi dropped me off at Steven's building on a busy corner in the West Village. I stepped over the sleeping black man in the foyer, rang the buzzer with no name on it (Steven would never put his name on a buzzer), and took the stairs to the second floor, where he

was waiting for me, peeking his head around the door.
He looked much better than I'd imagined, almost normal, really, except for a tiredness around his eyes, a
looseness in his muscles. Still, he was Steven, not
Steven's ghost.

He introduced me to his roommate, Ron, and friend
Seth, two more sweet, funny, good-looking single New
York guys (why couldn't I ever find one when I needed
one?). They were watching *Thelma and Louise* and waiting for their chicken parmigiana sandwiches to be delivered. I didn't know this was out on video, I exclaimed.

It wasn't video, these serious film buffs explained to
me. It was a laser disc, and furthermore, it was letter-
boxed, meaning that the picture was framed in a black
border so that the image on the TV had the same proportions as on a movie screen. In fact, the sound and the
picture were incredibly rich and clear. I was impressed.
Steven and I subsequently made several trips to the only
store in New York that rents these discs, and the weekend was filled with movies and sophisticated movie talk.
During intermission, I went through stacks of delivery
menus and ordered every kind of ethnic takeout my
heart desired.

Don't you think it's weird how I'm always friends
with really smart people? Steven asked, as we tried to
decide between the letter-boxed laser disc versions of
Manhunter and *The Maltese Falcon.*

That's because you're really smart too, I told him.

Nah, he said.

*   *   *

Sunday afternoon, Steven dozed off during his two-hour session with the intravenous-medicine pump. Ron was out, and I was looking around the apartment for something to do. I had been reading Amy Tan's *The Kitchen God's Wife* on the plane, but at that moment I didn't think I could move my consciousness all the way to China. I checked out Steven's bookcase, topped by a jungle of plants and jammed with cassette tapes. I knew without looking what they were: half ultrahip dance music and half the sweet sexy soul stuff Steven has such a weakness for. He'd never been a big reader; the only books I found were an art book on graffiti in SoHo that included photos of Steve's T-shirts, and a copy of *Rush*, the novel-turned-film of a lady narc gone astray. After a few chapters, I realized I'd be better off in China than with IV drug abusers.

I stared out the window at the people moving in and out of the deli across the street. Newspapers, candy bars, bottles of beer in paper sacks. I found myself thinking back to a call I received from my mother a couple of years ago, saying my grandmother was very ill. She said, If you want to see her again, you will have to come soon. I flew up that weekend with my three-month-old son.

Those two days in the hospital room, I found myself talking, talking endlessly, to the other visitors, even if Gigi wasn't listening. I was there with my baby and my talking, as if I could fill that quiet room with life, that plain, damp, rosewater-smelling room where my grandmother and another woman lay dying.

The first day my grandmother tried to keep up her end of the chatter, as she had all her life, when she was the biggest talker of them all. I brought the baby close to her and she smiled at him, and she reached with her swollen arms to touch his baby skin. She wouldn't kiss him, wouldn't breathe on him, as if what had gone wrong with her insides were contagious, or perhaps just unlucky.

The woman in the next bed, without visitors while my grandmother had six at a time, had a terrible cough. A ragged, harsh cough we winced to hear. I think my grandmother was embarrassed to be subjecting her visitors to this frightening sound, embarrassed that death was so near, that we could not just drink coffee and smoke cigarettes and eat Hershey's Kisses from her candy dish as always. Finally she was too tired to be embarrassed and she closed her eyes. I remember there was a huge box of dried fruit someone had brought—wet figs filled with tiny seeds, tart, shiny apricots, dates dusted with sugar and wrapped in gold paper—and we visitors began to eat the fruit like starving people.

I had never before consciously said good-bye for the last time, never kissed someone I loved, knowing there would not be another chance. Are you scared? I asked her. My voice sounded like a child's.

No, not scared, she said, just sad to leave you all,

and then she started to cry, and I did too. I left that day on an airplane and a week later she was gone.

Mar, said Steven. He was sitting up in bed watching me. What are you thinking about?

The last time I saw Gigi, I said, and a look crossed his face. Partly it was because he loved Gigi too, and partly because he knew why I was thinking about it.

It is one thing to lose your eighty-four-year-old grandmother, but it is quite another to face the death of your thirty-four-year-old friend. Maybe that's why I had to go see Steven when I did, to try to begin to accept it, to start mourning while there was still a chance to translate my grief into love and caring for a person who was there to receive it. But to be honest, I didn't accept it that weekend and I don't accept it today. You can make it, Steven, I kept telling him; it's not over till it's over.

Of course he argued with me.

I try not to get too excited when I hear he's returned to work, that the eye problem seems to have stabilized, that he's feeling better. I say prayers, I wish on stars and dandelions, and because I don't believe prayers and wishes alone will save all the people who face this merciless disease, I go to rallies, I write letters, and I give money. And every morning when I pick up the newspaper I look for the headline I see in my dreams: AIDS CURE.

The Out-of-Towners

Back when I was teaching writing to kids in East Austin, a student named Olivia Serrano asked if I went to church. No, I said, I'm Jewish.

What's that? she asked.

What do you think it is?

Someone from out of town? she guessed.

She was not far off. I don't live in the place where I grew up, literally or otherwise. To my parents' dismay if not surprise, I failed to find a nice Jewish guy—need I say doctor?—and to settle down in a nice suburb near my nice family. No, I married an Italian Catholic ice skater from Philadelphia and moved 1,732 miles away. I have one kid who babytalks with a heavy drawl and another whose favorite food is refried beans, a delicacy utterly unknown to the dining-room table at 7 Dwight Drive, West Deal, New Jersey.

College was my first chance to leave home, and I jumped at it. I sent for applications to schools in Chicago and California, but my parents said I had to stay on the East Coast. The one time they'd let me travel west of Trenton, I'd come home chanting mantras and carrying a suitcase full of incense and pictures of Lord Krishna. In any case, they were paying, so I had to obey.

The first close friend I made at school in Rhode Island was a girl named Jennifer from Dallas, and to my great excitement she invited me to spend spring break at her parents' home. We sat under the magnolia tree and drank Diet Dr Pepper out of long-neck bottles. Later we went to a bar and drank Lone Star beer out of long-neck bottles. Then we drove down to Austin, where it was April, everyone was twenty, and there were pickup trucks and long-neck bottles everywhere we went. I was in love.

I had never seen a city with trees before. I had never seen quite so electric a green. I had never bought a doughnut at a drive-up window, had a nacho, or gotten a headache from drinking a sweet frozen drink too fast. Hell, back home we didn't even have twenty-four-hour convenience stores.

Within days, I was obsessed with the desire to own a dog, the bigger the better, and a pickup truck, and boots, and a cowboy hat. I rushed down to the Goodwill to work on my new wardrobe and discovered a pair of elaborately stitched Tony Lamas, already broken in, exactly my size. Aren't these the greatest boots? I demanded, showing off my purchase. They have wizard toes! Eventually someone took pity on me and pointed out that I had misread the hand-lettered tag: they had lizard toes, not wizard toes. Oh well.

And barbecue! Yum! Too bad I was a vegetarian. Undaunted, I ate pickle-and-onion sandwiches on white bread slathered with barbecue sauce and accompanied by a pile of potato salad. It was the sweet smoky atmosphere I lusted after, anyway, not the brisket—that and the young cowboys hunkered down at the counter, ordering plates of ribs in deep, slow voices I could barely understand. Equally dangerous food-and-men experiences occurred in Mexican restaurants, where the *huevos* were hot and the waiters were hotter.

When I returned East, I couldn't help but notice that my part of the country seemed to lack regional mystique. Even James Michener was not interested in our state history. We did not drink "Garden State" Beer. We did not wear "Native New Jerseyite" T-shirts. We did not know what our state flag looked like and certainly did not care to affix its replica to the bumpers of our cars. Secede? As in saw off our little peninsula full of alienated suburbs, desperate cities, and invisible farms and float out into the Atlantic? You must be joking.

The Texans, on the other hand, were quite content with their sunny acres. Born in Texas, they would live in Texas and die in Texas; many hoped to stay on for the afterlife as well. This fascinated me. I transplanted myself among them, no less a convert than Sammy Davis, Jr.

Both my children are native Texans, but where you are born is more than a physical place. After all, they are half Jewish, and in these parts, Jewish means from out of town; I don't think their Italian Catholic half wears cowboy boots either. Everything Tony and I know about who we are, where we come from, we got by osmosis. But down here, neither Jewish nor Italian comes in the water.

My parents' Jewishness was much more about lifestyle than about faith. They belonged to a Jewish country club, they ate bagels and lox on the weekends, they gave money for trees to be planted in Israel. My father wouldn't have dreamed of working on Yom Kippur. In fact, to this day my mother calls every year to see if I'm planning to work on Yom Kippur. There's something about the Day of Atonement that gets to even the most nonobservant Jews, among whom my parents were certainly numbered. They did not go to services, had only one set of china, off which they ate both bacon and lobster, and (this was pretty wild, even in their assimilated crowd) gave presents on Christmas. When the time came, they hastily joined a temple so Nancy and I could attend Hebrew school.

At first, I loved it. I planned to move to Israel and become a rabbi as soon as possible. But then, at thirteen, just weeks before my bat mitzvah, I stormed out of there for good. I was an atheist! Okay, maybe an agnostic. Certainly not a hypocrite like my parents, who never got closer to the temple than the curb out front, when it was their turn to drive the carpool. If she doesn't have to go, I'm not going either, said Nancy. She later married an Italian guy too.

Tony's religious background had a little more religion in it than mine. On Sunday, all the members of his family, or the female ones, at least, went to church, where Tony was an altar boy. He was named after a saint, learned the principles of penmanship from sisters in swooshing black skirts, and ate fish every Friday. But sometime during his teens, he strayed from the fold.

Maybe it was when his mother, divorcing a cruel philanderer, was excommunicated by the church she needed more than ever. Maybe the Catholic worldview just stopped making sense. Perhaps he had secretly hated fish all along. In any case, by the time I met him, he was not a candidate for the Ten Most Catholic list. Now he likes to dress up as a nun for Halloween and offer spiritual guidance on issues like whether there should be meat in lasagna, and which is better, Parmesan or Romano.

Even if you're not religious, when you marry within your ethnic group, you tend to preserve the basic traditions. You have your wedding in a church or temple. You do certain things on certain holidays. When your kids are old enough, you give them the same religious education you had, if only to provide something to rebel against.

Our wedding was held in a golf club and was performed by a mayor. It mentioned God in a nice nondenominational way. At the end, my groom smashed a glass Jewish style; one of my new cousins later presented me with a needlepoint wall hanging of a cross stitched with our names and the wedding date.

We are occasionally invited to seders and latke parties by our Jewish friends. We eat seven different kinds of fish on Christmas Eve at Tony's grandma's. Tony sometimes sounds like a Lower East Side homeboy, putzing around with his tchotchkes and kvetching about his tsuris. I, on the other hand, delight in shopping for excessively Christian greeting cards for his older relatives. May Your Eightieth Birthday Be Filled with the Love of Jesus; please send me your recipe for manicotti. Rumor has it that in the extreme throes of childbirth, I called for assistance from the Holy Mother of God.

The arrival of children has made it all more complex. For example, the penis thing. Tony was in favor of circumcision on general principles, so that much was easy. We could ignore the growing fad for intact foreskins. Then, right before Hayes was born, I witnessed a lovely Jewish naming ceremony for the baby daughter of some friends. I thought about giving Hayes a bris, a ritual Jewish circumcision. After all, by Jewish law, the child of a Jewish woman is Jewish, no matter what. And

I wanted to ask God's blessings for him somehow. Is a little tradition such a terrible thing?

Then I had a talk with myself. Marion, I said, you've never even *been* to a bris. You don't belong to a temple, you don't know a rabbi, you don't know ten Jewish people in Austin for the minyan. If you become such a big Jew now, you're a hypocrite! Jewish law or no Jewish law, half this kid's family is Catholic. They probably believe that he can't get into heaven unless he's baptized.

Okay, no bris. No baptism either. What's wrong with a nice simple birth certificate?

A few years ago, I had an argument with my uncle and his wife. She is an orthodox Moroccan Jew. Although he once had little interest in Judaism, since his marriage he has embraced the faith with zeal, conducting the Sabbath dinner every Friday like an old hand. He wears a yarmulke; she lights candles. Their children attend a Jewish parochial school. But, I assumed out loud, you would never be the type of parents who would disown their daughter because she married a non-Jew, I said.

The wife's face fell. What Hitler couldn't do with the camps, Jews are doing to themselves with intermarriage, my uncle told me.

I was shocked. But what about the melting pot? I

asked. Didn't you see *West Side Story*? Isn't love more important than tribal allegiance? Isn't tribal allegiance one step away from racism?

We don't get in the melting pot, said the wife, because we don't want to melt.

You know it's December in Texas when tamale fixin's go on special at the grocery store. Tony goes out to buy Hanukkah candles and I am dispatched to find The Tree. A box full of ornaments, stockings, and Advent calendars arrives from Tony's mother; the house is already festooned with the Feliz Navidad cutouts we bought in Laredo.

Normally I am pretty cranky at this time of year, but as the kids get older, it's hard to resist their enthusiasm. They know every Christmas carol backwards and forwards, thanks to the Sri Lankan director of their Montessori school. They believe in Santa Claus, which I quickly determined has useful disciplinary implications. Hayes lights the menorah with aplomb, and even Vincie joins in on the last few words of the blessing.

Christmas Eve, we're up past three A.M. wrapping presents. I in my kerchief, Tony in his cap; the children refuse to settle down for their long winter's nap until after midnight. Just hours later, they are wide-awake and ecstatic and all the wrapping paper we just put on is torn off. People come over in the afternoon for vegetarian shepherd's pie. The kids are naked and swim-

ming in the hot tub when our Syrian American friend
Tom Mallouk arrives in his Santa Claus costume and
hands gifts from his sack into their dripping hands. This
worked great last year, but this time his six-year-old
daughter cannot be fooled. It's not Santa Claus, she
says. It's Daddy.

Hayes isn't sure. At bedtime he still has several
questions. Was it Santa Claus or was it Tom? What
about the guy in the robe with the sheep on the Christmas card—is that God? And how come we don't go to
church?

Because Mommy's from out of town, I joke, but I
know he doesn't get it. Then I tell him the truth as best
I can.

A Night in New Orleans

had never kept a secret from Tony before. Had I ever
kept a secret at all? To me, "Don't tell anybody" never
really meant "Don't tell *anybody*." But for once it was
my secret, not somebody else's, and the better I kept
it, the more delicious it would be when revealed. I tell
you, it was a struggle. All through the month leading up
to the surprise I had planned for Tony's thirty-fourth
birthday, I lay in bed each night, unable to get to sleep,
mulling over the details in my mind. After finally dozing
off, I would awaken a few hours later, the secret pressing on my chest, running through my veins. I felt like
Raskolnikov. I felt like an adulteress.

Not that I didn't talk about it all. God, no. In fact,
I told so many people—friends, relatives, co-workers,
perfect strangers—about my plans, the secret seemed to
become a palpable presence, a hum in the air. Couldn't

he hear it? Wouldn't the knowledge seep in through his pores? When I was with Tony, virtually every thought that went through my head was one I had to keep to myself. I had never known such self-censorship nor had any idea I was capable of it. I would sit there at the dinner table, no sooner opening my mouth to speak than shutting it again, once bursting into laughter with the absurd effort of it all.

What's so funny? demanded Tony.

Oh, I just thought of something that happened.

What?

Something at work . . . I can't explain it. I mean . . . it's not really that funny.

Are you feeling all right? he asked skeptically.

Toward the end, I was literally counting the hours. I phoned the babysitters I had lined up to stay with our one- and three-year-old sons several times a day. I ran out repeatedly for one more bunch of bananas, another Disney video. I arranged to have Tony spirited off to *Terminator II* the final evening so I would have time to pack, hide the suitcases, and run around the house in a baseball cap checking off my encyclopedic lists, as if we were leaving for thirty days, not thirty hours.

The appointed Saturday morning finally arrived. His actual birthday had come and gone earlier that week, with enough fuss on my part to allay any suspicion. From seven A.M. to ten-fifteen I managed to maintain an air of intense normalcy. At that moment, according to plan, babysitter number one pulled into the driveway.

Say good-bye to the kids, I told Tony. He looked at me as if his recent doubts about my mental health had finally come to a head.

We had driven about halfway to the airport when I couldn't take it another minute. Don't you know where we're going? I asked him. The route we were taking led to only two places, and the other was Quality Seafood Market.

To the airport? he said in a tone of wonder.

Yes, I said, and handed him an envelope containing the tickets.

If there was ever a town made for meeting one's true love, it is New Orleans. If you even think you might fall, the whole city conspires to push you over the edge. Bring on the lush subtropical climate, the heartrending saxophone, the moonlit path by the river. Wheel in the masked revelers, the drunken abandon, the voodoo drumbeat. Roll out the satiny oysters, the artichoke hearts, the beignets in their drifts of sugar, the cafés and bars and clubs open all night long.

New Orleans cast her spell on me the day I crossed the city limits for the first time. I wound up hopelessly in love with the first man I laid eyes on. It was February 8, 1983, and I was twenty-four years old. I pulled into town at dawn in a small blue car packed with stiff, sweaty, overcaffeinated Mardi Gras celebrants-to-be. We had come eighteen hundred miles from the heart of

Manhattan over the Smokies through the bluegrass to the bayou. Now our handwritten directions led us off I-10 down St. Charles Avenue, past the regally porched and pillared mansions lining the boulevard, the old-fashioned streetcar gliding down its grassy median.

Just a few blocks off St. Charles we found the Garden District address where our friends Shelley and Pete had rented a tiny two-room apartment, offered as carnival headquarters for their East Coast pals. The door was answered by a tall good-looking guy I didn't know. The way I remember it, I walked in, said hello, and sat on his lap. Eventually, we were introduced. My new interest in life was Shelley and Pete's longtime friend Tony from Philadelphia. He had been living in New Orleans for five years, teaching ice-skating. Upon finding himself unexpectedly between apartments and jobs and relationships, this funny, elegant, unconventional, and slightly wild young man had moved in temporarily with his old friends.

Within an hour we were parked by the levee, playing "Do Ya Wanna Funk" on the cassette deck, a case of Mardi Gras–brand beer in the backseat. I was hanging out the sunroof in the white Louisiana morning, singing, as huge boats slipped down the gray Mississippi to the Gulf. Less than two months later, I had abandoned my life in New York City and was living with Tony on Royal Street in the French Quarter.

It was a stormy and decadent time. Neither of us worked much, or slept much, or spent many days completely sober. For me, this was pretty much par for the course. For nearly a decade, a series of calamitous loves had begun with similar passion and intensity, though each had its own uniquely tragic end. Why this one actually worked out, how we weathered our excesses, stayed together, turned into adults, and wound up ten years later in Austin, Texas, with two kids and two cars and one last name, I'm not quite sure. I have to assume destiny had a hand in it.

I feel like Cinderella, said Tony as we stepped out of the terminal in New Orleans with our overnight bags. All my scheming had been worth it: he was completely surprised and thrilled. Even the airplane ride was a treat, the first time we'd flown without kids in what felt like forever. We actually read books, and talked, and balanced full glasses on our tray tables without fear.

To choose a hotel Tony would approve of, I had cooked up a story that a woman I worked with was dating an indulgent older man who planned to whisk her off for a weekend in New Orleans. Where should I tell them to stay? I'd innocently queried. Now, stepping out of our taxi at a small hotel at the quiet end of the French Quarter, he put two and two together.

So, he said wryly, I guess Donna Bell's not really going to New Orleans.

No, I replied, a little sad for her, and she doesn't have a boyfriend either.

No matter how charming the French Quarter looks from the street, its rarest treasures are hidden from public view. Behind almost any pair of tall wooden doors lurks a cool, shadowy carriageway opening on a sunstruck courtyard blooming with banana trees and bougainvillea, furbished with wrought-iron furniture and flagstones. Our hotel room was located in a shady corner of just such a secret Eden. Inside, pale yellow draperies with a delicate floral pattern swept from the high ceiling to the foot of the French doors.

Even before we saw the jacuzzi in the bathroom and the lavishly stocked bar, we had decided to spend the afternoon in our room. Suffice it to say we had not spent a Saturday afternoon alone in three years, and there was some concern that we might have to wait another three before it happened again. Eventually, knowing our dinner reservations were not until nine, we wandered out on the streets of the Quarter, drawn as always to the intoxicating brew of dignity and tackiness, grandeur and raunch, that is New Orleans.

Surrounded by the babble of tourists, we stopped at the old familiar places: Café du Monde for café au lait, Central Grocery for a sandwich to go. The streets themselves were like friends to us. As we had every lazy day of the months we lived there, we strolled between the long poles that hold up the second-floor balconies, feeling as if scenes out of Tennessee Williams or Anne Rice might be going on above our heads.

I felt knocked over with love for Tony. Part of it, I

think, was the sudden unrestricted access to the well of emotion that is normally sucked almost dry by the raising of children. My arms, usually so full of babies and groceries and dinner plates, kept reaching for him. I knew the kids were fine (I had already called, of course), so I let them go for a while, and reveled in being two instead of four, in feeling like lovers instead of harried but friendly business partners. I had wondered, those nights lying awake, if an experience so calculated for romance could really be romantic. Believe me, I wondered no more.

Around two in the morning, the night man at the hotel brought us champagne on a tray. We toasted Shelley and Pete, New Orleans, each other, our kids, our parents, our babysitter.

Privately, I also drank to the fact that I really could keep a secret if I wanted to, which was an interesting and dangerous thing to know.

My Secret Crush

The day I met you at Leah's garage sale, there were so many questions I wanted to ask. Do you have a girlfriend? Is it serious? Are you married? Is it serious? Do you like my hair this way? Do you think intelligent women are sexy? I've read that some people do, but maybe that's only in books. I could change for you, darling, it's nothing, I've done it before. They work wonders today with simple shots and surgery. I could shave my legs for you, even. I once renounced shaving on principle, but now my legs are just something to stand on, their texture of little concern to anyone. You could change all that in a minute. I could be smooth for you. I could draw the silver blade along my shinbone with exquisite care. I would bleed for you, darling, tiny cuts pinking the bathwater, but if it was for you, I would be porcelain, I would be glass.

I want to open your refrigerator, try on your clothes, listen to the messages on your answering machine. I want to find the worn pages in your atlas and take you away. Did you use to smoke cigarettes? Vodka or scotch? Morning or night, gentle or rough, fast or slow?

I had a dream the other night. We were at the movies, you and I, both accompanied by other people. The film was *Putney Swope*—I recognized the part where the braless black stewardesses are jumping on a trampoline. You didn't see me, but I was just across the aisle, watching your face in the reflected light, your low, ticklish laugh, your comments to your companion, your hand on the arm of the chair, which could have been my leg. After the show there was quite a melee in the lobby; I was set adrift from my life and washed up at your feet. Then you bent as if to kiss me and I felt the back of my neck untie, a shiver along the inside of my mouth. A long time went by, the time of seven dreams, seven showings of *Putney Swope*, and we were still there.

The next time I saw you in real life, sitting in that restaurant by yourself, I half-thought the dream was true. My lips parted in spite of me, wet and involuntary. I had a dream about you, I said, my voice husky with passion. Are you all right? you said. Do you have a sore throat?

Last week I bought a used novel at the thrift store. When I opened it, a small gift card, once used as a bookmark, fluttered out. *Gorgeous*, it said, *won't you wear this next Sunday night when we go out to dinner?*

I can't wait. Your guy. I read that note over and over. I studied the handwriting. And kept it by the side of my bed like a match near a tinderbox.

The main thing is, I don't want to ruin our friendship. I know it's not much of a friendship, but if I say something to you like Feel how soft the skin is on the inside of my thigh, that's going to be the end of it right there. I'll never be able to shop at Safeway again. Okay, I admit I didn't use to go to that Safeway, it's not exactly on my way home, but I'm used to shopping there now. I'm used to searching the parking lot for your car. I'm used to strolling along the back wall of the store, trying to see which aisle you might be in. Hello, I say, passing you casually, lifting a can of shaving cream off the shelf. Hi! you say, how's it going?

Oh, fine, I say, and you? Would you like to come over to my house and eat butter lettuce? I could make you a wonderful soup with coconut milk. We could watch *60 Minutes*. I could show you my aquarium. But how would I keep from staring at your shoulders, your wonderful thick arms, your unknown hands? Hey, I would say shyly, turning off the sound on Andy Rooney. Do you think—would you like me to rub your back?

You know, my biggest problem with shaving has always been how often you have to do it. Leah says it depends on if it's for looks or for feel. For looks, once a week. For feel, every day. Okay then, every day, no, twice a day, first thing and last, for you!

Thirty-five

ast year, on her thirty-fifth birthday, my friend Anita
pulled up in front of my house in a stretch limousine
wearing a glamorous charcoal gray sweaterdress and
drinking shots of expensive tequila with her new girlfriend, Lorraine. We were shocked. Not by the fact of
the girlfriend; that was old news. But the dress, the car,
the tequila—this was not the casual yuppie Anita we
used to know, the Anita of jeans and Topsiders and
Amstel Light. Out of the blue she turns up with this
tequila-drinking, cashmere-wearing, limo-renting gal at
her side, as if it's all as familiar and natural as her
well-thumbed copy of the L. L. Bean catalog.

Looking back on this incident from the far side of my
own thirty-fifth birthday, I realize Anita was just kicking
off her midlife crisis. Since I've been having one myself,
I can recognize it a mile away. One day you're sitting

there, innocently filling out some survey, and it wants to know if you are sixteen to twenty, twenty-one to twenty-five, twenty-six to thirty, thirty-one to thirty-four, or thirty-five and over. Thirty-five and over? As if it's the end of the line, as if youth with its many gradations and graduations is behind you and from here on out it's a done deal, a blur, a straight shot through middle age until you collect your IRAs, become an official senior citizen, and get discounts at the movies and the cafeteria.

What are they, nuts? Of course you can still change. Just because a few of the impulsive decisions you made back in your twenties had a little more staying power than others, and now here you are, ten years later, with the same partner, the same children, the same job, the same address, the same phone number, the same friends and enemies—surely that doesn't mean fate is through with you and nothing new will ever happen again. All these responsibilities you have and commitments you've made—surely there's still some freedom, some spontaneity, a couple of unknown quantities lurking behind Doors Number One and Two.

Last year, my friend Mike started doing chin-ups and had an E-mail romance with a sociology grad student in Madison. A former housemate cut back her law practice to open a catering business and started sleeping with her partner on the side; she and her husband split up and got back together three times in one year. The woman I worked for sold her half of the business

and took up channeling screenplays from departed spir-
its and attending codependent self-help groups. She
hired Ron the Closet Queen to redo her wardrobe and
was recently seen in purple leather shorts and zebra-
striped high heels.

I myself managed to turn my life upside down and
my soul inside out over what was essentially an adolescent infatuation. With someone who had barely emerged
from adolescence himself. In a ridiculously short time,
I lost thirty pounds, took up bike riding and lying to my
husband, and started wearing tiny silver hoops in my
ears and carrying a backpack instead of a purse. I
changed brands of cigarettes, developed a taste for
Guinness Stout, and even considered folk dancing.

Lust is usually the key element in these second-act
transformations. All the incredible effort people put into
trying to change themselves and reform their habits, and
then they fall in love or lust and get a new personality
overnight. But is it possible to combine the act of making more or less of an ass of oneself with some meaningful and enduring change?

If the impetus is to feel young and free again, the
best thing I got out of my little episode was a twenty-
one-speed turquoise bicycle. The person I was at ten or
eleven years old—I can feel her inside me as I fly down
the hills with the wind in my face. No matter how late I
am, I don't hurry; I can't get there significantly faster, so
why bother. Bike riding has changed my relationship to
the weather as well. Once, I had no special appreciation

for cool gray mornings. My love of a warm breeze was intellectual. Now we are quite intimate, as it lifts the buttoned edge of my blouse and slides around my waist.

Thinking is different on a bicycle, less linear, more luxurious. The ride to my office is half an hour long, and sometimes I think about the same thing for the whole ride. I used to think that I never thought. I just recycled experiences through my mind, as if suffering from some endless hangover from which I could recover only by piecing events and conversations together in order, re-winding and replaying them over and over again. The only time I could recognize evidence of actual thinking was when I was talking. I would hear myself voicing ideas and opinions I didn't know I had and would realize later that was it! Now I can see that I do think, after all, and even with my mouth shut. It is not necessarily a goal-oriented thing. I don't come away with some pre-cious jewel of insight every day. Or any day. Just a feeling of what it is like inside my mind, a place where no one interrupts me and the phone never rings.

If there is indeed such a thing as changing at this semilate date in life, the eventual outcome of the pro-cess remains a mystery. Are we becoming something that already exists inside us, an abiding true self, which is gradually revealed? Opening like a rosebud, unfold-ing like a plot, mutating like a horror-movie monster? Is there progress toward an endpoint other than where we began, the real person, the butterfly? Or do we just zigzag like sine waves, cycle endlessly like the seasons, degenerate in amorphous entropy like the universe or like our physical bodies themselves?

Take a guy who gets back from Vietnam and spends ten years in the basement of an apartment building in Harlem, shooting junk and drinking cases of cheap beer. Eventually he pulls himself together and becomes a drug-and-alcohol-abuse counselor with a sunny apartment and a sleek red car. He sets up housekeeping with my divorced sister and forbids her to wear low-cut blouses in public. You can't really say he fits into any one of these models because God only knows what's going to happen next.

I've made some of the biggest decisions of my life just to see what would happen next. Seven years ago, I announced that the reason I was getting married was to have a big party with everyone I love and drink champagne and laugh all day. That was partly true, but it was more that I wanted to see how getting married would change me, would change Tony, would change us. As scary as it sounds, I felt the same way about having children.

The day I turned thirty-five, in a burst of hopeful energy and possibility, I sat down and wrote a huge long list of resolutions and wishes. When I finished, I realized it was the same list I've been making for years. As usual, if it were up to me, I would be good-hearted and beautiful and generous and patient and creative, have excellent muscle tone, a clean house, and a decent car. There would be world peace and an end to hunger and a cure for AIDS. I'm superstitious about wishing. I always put a few big altruistic ones in there so my fairy godmother, or whoever is on the grant committee that evaluates the worthiness of wishes and their wishers, won't think I'm selfish. I never wish for everyone I love to be safe, and for no calamities or creeping evils to befall us. A wish like that is dangerous, a monkey's paw, a flouting of fate. So I wish instead for the strength to play the cards I am dealt.

A couple of weeks ago, my ex-brother-in-law, Steven, died, two days after observing the passage of his thirty-sixth year in St. Vincent's Hospital in New York City. Days later, our babysitter's new love went down in a two-seater plane. God knows what happened in Bosnia that week, or Somalia, or the West Bank, or up the road in Waco. Or what is happening right now in the cells of the bodies of the people I love. If I make it to forty-five and fifty-five, and beyond, something tells me, I will look back on this time and laugh. Or maybe cry. Because nothing will be the same. Because thirty-five is not about stopping but about the fear of stopping, and all that it drives us to, all that it brings down on our heads.

Things Don't Just Disappear

oday we are looking for my car keys, a pair of sunglasses, the baby's yellow swim trunks. In addition to
today's specials, we are, as always, keeping an eye
out for my driver's license and video club card, mis-
cellaneous kitchen utensils, earrings, and small wooden
toys, the one pacifier preferred above all others, the personal statement I wrote when I applied to law school five
or ten years ago. Whatever made me think to look for that
old thing and, finding it gone, spend the rest of the summer searching and mourning? As if I had lost the young,
earnest part of me that wrote it.

We are tearing apart the house, going through drawers and file cabinets and toy chests. Checking the dump-
ster, the laundry hamper, the refrigerator. One time we
found a missing scissors in the egg compartment. A
string of pearls in the recycling bin. We will not rest; we

cannot think of anything else. Why are we always looking for things, asks Tony wearily. He sounds as if he's
about to cry.

As a person who naturally maintains a warm, solicitous relationship with the material objects in his life,
he cannot fathom the stubborn streak of carelessness to
which the afflicted state of my possessions bears wit-
ness. If they are not lost altogether, my things are
stained or scratched or broken, in sad and urgent need
of cleaning and mending. *His* things are well taken care
of, polished, folded, neatly stored. They don't go flying
out of his pocket, slipping into the garbage, jumping
into somebody else's car. They stick to him like glue.

The only thing that sticks with me is a kind of fitful,
half-baked antimaterialism, an impatience with the tyr-
anny of objects. Because of it, I just don't notice what
kind of car other people drive, or the puddle I'm about
to step into, or where I set down my bag when I got
home. And this leaves the door wide open to the cold
wind of chaos, which sweeps through my life at unpredictable intervals to exact its toll. There wasn't a bone
in my body that wanted to lose my heirloom engagement
ring two weeks after it was given to me. I only wore it to
a party on the outside of a glove because I wanted to be
able to look at it all night long. And then it was days
before my husband-to-be could drag me out of the
hedges and pry the rented metal detector from my frozen
hands.

If objects I actually cherish are not exempt from the

curse, the outlook is grimmer still for things for which I feel no love. In early adolescence, for example, I lost seven or eight pairs of eyeglasses in one year. I dropped them in the street while hurrying to the bus stop and found them run over on the way home, a million sparkly blue plastic pieces on the pavement. I accidentally put them in my lunch bag with the remainder of a baloney sandwich and flicked the whole thing into the trash. My mother telephoned the school in a panic; a janitor was dispatched to go through the incinerator. One pair after the next, those glasses flew off my face and out of my life, propelled by some strange centrifugal force.

Back then, my looking was all for show. I'll search the bedroom, Ma, I'd call, and take one quick peek in the closet. Then I'd flop on the bed with a magazine till she came to check on me. I looked everywhere, I'd tell her. They're gone. I pictured something in the way of a distant galaxy, where tennis balls, orthodontic retainers, geography books, combs, and puppies rotated slowly in the luminous violet air. Whoosh, my glasses were sucked in by a powerful vacuum. Zip, the entrance to the place seamed up like a tent.

My mother took a wholly different attitude. The fact that anything could be lost at all was an affront to her worldview. She put something away, it stayed there. If it didn't, she tracked it to the ends of the earth. She determined when it was last seen, where, and by whom. She lined up the usual suspects: me, my sister, the dog. Who took the good pen out of my purse? She pulled the refrigerator away from the wall; she carefully sorted through old newspapers. It's got to be somewhere, she muttered. Things don't just disappear.

When my family went to see the circus at Madison Square Garden, my mother lost a contact lens in the crowded cement passageway that led to our seats. Hold it! shouted my father, flat-palmed like a traffic cop, and a circular space cleared around us. Men, women, and children were down on their knees, nose to tail like elephants, seeking the tiny transparent circle on the dusty floor. My mother stood motionless in the center, scouting with her one working eye as my father patted down her woolen suit. I'm not related to them, I told anyone who would listen.

In my mother's opinion, to lose something due to carelessness was a sin that required penance. To atone for one's failure to keep track of one's little flock of objects, one had to devote oneself completely to the pursuit of the lost lamb, be it a ballpoint pen or a ten-dollar bill. Whatever it was, in becoming lost it achieved a significance far greater than any it had ever known.

Now I spend half my life blithely leaving restaurants without my purse or my jacket and the other half maniacally searching my house for the cat-food coupon I put away so carefully. For God's sake, Marion, says Tony three days into the drama, is it still that damn coupon? Of course not, I lie.

But sometimes the obsession pays off. Like the time

Hayes had his little friend Emily Rose over and they scattered every piece of every toy he owns from one end of the house to the other. When the dust settled, an octagonal green puzzle piece had completely disappeared. I called up Emily Rose's mother, Carole. Look in your diaper bag, I ordered.

But it wasn't in the diaper bag, or in our garbage disposal, or on the bookshelf, or in any of the thousand other places I looked in the weeks that followed. I called up the toy store the puzzle came from and inquired about ordering a replacement part. They laughed at me.

Then one day I was in the bathroom, thinking about nothing, looking at the hole in the wall that was made when the toilet paper holder fell off and took a big hunk of Sheetrock with it. Suddenly I had an inspiration. Reaching into the hole and down toward the floor, I brushed something with my fingertips. Could it be? I crammed in my arm up to the shoulder. Exultant, I called Tony at work. The green thing! I shouted.

That's great, he said. But what about the cat-food coupon?

And let us not forget the famous incident of Sandye's glove in Chinatown. Ever since we were in fifth grade, every time I borrowed something from Sandye I would lose it or break it or wreck it. After fifteen years of this she said, Enough. You better not borrow anything from me anymore.

Then Tony and I came up from Texas to visit her in

New York and it was a very cold day and I had no gloves and we hadn't seen each other in a while, so despite everything, she lent me a pair and sent us off for the afternoon. Imagine my horror a few hours later when one of my coat pockets was suddenly empty. We looked, we looked, we retraced our steps, we went back to Hong Fat, where we'd had lunch. By then, it had begun to grow dark.

It took forever to get out of Chinatown, rush-hour traffic two weeks before Christmas, streets and side-walks filled with people scurrying home. I was despon-dent in the backseat, staring out the window as if somehow the glove might appear. And against all prob-ability, it did. One wool-lined leather glove, returned from the ethers only slightly trampled, lying in the mid-dle of Mott Street. Tony, I cried out. Stop the car.

I keep at least a dozen pens in my purse at all times and force myself not to count them to make sure they're all there. I do not favor one over the others, for I know that will make it disappear. I never purposely hide a thing from myself, or put it in a safe and secret place. If I do, I will never see it again.

When my mother comes to visit, I lose something big, just to give us something to do. A credit card, my watch, the recipe for vinaigrette. Then we are overtaken by the rhythm of looking, like aging actors starring in a revival of their first hit show. Our lines come back as if it were yesterday. It'll turn up, don't worry. Oh, I know, I'm sure it will. Did you have it when you went to the supermarket? Have you already looked in the car?

At my father's funeral, my mother, my sister, and I were given small badges made from a piece of black grosgrain ribbon to wear during the period of mourning. The ribbon had a cut in it to symbolize the rending of garments traditionally performed by members of the bereaved Jewish family. I remember pinning the strange decoration on my dress with a kind of bitter pride.

Later that day or the next, in a noisy house filled with plates of food and vats of coffee and half-empty highball glasses, I looked down and saw the ribbon was gone. My hand flew up to my heart. It's okay, honey, said my mother, you can have mine. I don't want yours, I half-screamed at her, and went crazy, tearing up the house, crawling under the couch, yanking out drawers that hadn't been opened in years. Finally I threw myself on my childhood bed in despair.

Then Tony and Sandye burst into my room, all flushed with their little conspiracy, shouting, Look, Mar, it was in the car! It was in the car! Tony brandished a torn black ribbon, but I knew it wasn't mine. At first I wasn't going to take it. Then, as I looked at their eager, helpful faces, something gave in me. I wiped my eyes, pinned the false ribbon on my shirt, and did not search anymore. I took it home with me to Texas and placed it in my lingerie drawer, where it is at this very moment. I never look at it.

My first ribbon, the original ribbon, is somewhere in my mother's house. It will turn up. Unlike people, things don't just disappear.

My Sibilant Darling

W here's my brother? asks three-year-old Hayes when I pick him up at the preschool. (You should see him, Nancy. He's a big boy now. He can write his name.) He cranes his neck to check the baby seat in the back of the car. Is he at home? Is he waiting for me? Did Daddy give him a popsicle?

When we pull up, his little brother is on the front porch. As Vince recognizes the car, a flock of emotions flies across his year-old face. His happiness at seeing me is edged with pain because the joy of my arrival reminds him how sad it is that I wasn't there just a moment ago. And how endless the path from the street to the house! How long until I lift him in my arms! But then he notices his big brother racing up the steps ahead of me, and you can see it happen: the registering, the shift of attention. The airwaves open up. *He's here.* Each

of them subtly changes into what they are when they are
together. Brother first, everything else after.

We want a banana, Hayes says. I want one, and my
brother wants one too. And they run to the kitchen,
laughing because running to the kitchen is funny. In the
same way splashing all the water out of the bathtub is
funny. In a few years, it will be making fart noises with
their lips in the backseat of the car.

And now the big one builds a tower of blocks and the
little one knocks it over. Incensed, the builder smacks
the innocent toppler, who bursts into tears and toddles
off crying. No! Don't leave, shouts his big brother, grab-
bing him and dragging him back. Play with this, he
says, solicitously presenting a broken piece of some
dead toy. And the baby is smiling, honored, waving the
plastic turtle foot over his head like an Olympic trophy.

When each of these boys was born, I looked into
their deep blue eyes and saw you, my Nancypants. You
were the first baby I ever knew.

Yes, I was the big sister. I was always right, I was
always first, I always knew more. Of every enterprise, I
was the president, CEO, and chairman. To find things I
could not do better, you had to stretch. You had to press
your hands and feet against opposite walls of the corri-
dor and climb up to the ceiling. Then you would come
down the hall like that, spread-eagled, inching along
over my head, one hand, one foot at a time.

When they had company, our parents liked to show
off our accomplishments. I recited my poems, played

"Für Elise" on the piano, drew pastel portraits of everyone at the table. And you—the pretty one, the quiet one, the cute little blond one who, legend has it, used to fit in the milk box, for whom diet pills, braces, or a nose job would never even be suggested—you climbed the walls. The guests were dumbstruck.

Our parents did their best to treat us fairly. We wore the same part in our hair, the same Danskin outfits, rode identical pink bicycles with handlebar baskets. We went to the same Hebrew school and ballet school and took piano lessons in adjoining half hours from the decrepit Mrs. Baumbach. But really, wasn't it me who taught you everything? How to write, read, and add, all the countries and their crops, how to play house, how to ride a bike, even how to masturbate with a stuffed rabbit. I snagged a library book called *The Magic Garden of Stanley Sweetheart* off Mommy's night table and made you vocabulary lists of swear words, had you spell each one and use it in a sentence.

We shared a daisy-papered bedroom, shelves full of dolls and chemistry sets, a billion bottles of Tab. Daddy taught us the foolproof way to split a soda: one pours, the other picks. Sharing people was a little more complex. Some of our bitterest battles were fought over our neighbor Carolyn Mahoney, in whose home Welch's grape juice flowed like water. Even in elementary school, one sister had only to miss the school bus and the other would swoop in on the prey, huddling with Car in the last row, plying her with schemes and secrets.

Then you finally succeeded in stealing her away, and you and she and Donna Benoit kept secret journals documenting my various appalling faux pas. *My sister had her shirt on backwards today. She is so queer*, you wrote.

Perhaps exhausted with the effort of competition, you spent most of your ninth year in bed with mononucleosis and appendicitis. This left me with Carolyn and Donna but no sweet taste of victory. *Nancy's life has become an endless parade of hospitals and presents*, I wrote to our grandmother Gigi at Christmas. *Her teacher comes to the house, but only twice a week. She lives by herself in the playroom, and has her own bathroom and TV.*

As we tumbled into puberty, our parents deemed that we would have our own bedrooms. A decorator was hired to help us select wallpaper, carpeting, and furniture. The boudoir of my dreams featured an electric green shag rug and op art concentric squares radiating from the ceiling. Failing to present a concept of your own, you were assigned a Pennsylvania Dutch flowered scheme. Within a year, you had repapered the walls with Alice Cooper posters and devoted hours of Sistine Chapelesque toil to the mosaic of empty red-and-white Marlboro boxes covering the ceiling. This was the new Nancy, one who sewed dozens and dozens of patches on a pair of disintegrating blue jeans and refused to wear anything else. You were out of the milk box for good.

By this time, our early teens, the more obvious rivalry between us had ceased. Not that we were fooled by the parental affirmative action programs. There was no doubt that I was smarter and you were cuter. Instead of hating each other, we began to merge our assets. I shared everything I had: friends, secrets, records, rides to concerts. When you occasionally failed to do the same, I could get mean, spilling the beans to Mommy when you lost your virginity or letting you catch me with your boyfriend on the golf course. What a terrible, thrilling betrayal, his Mick Jagger lips on mine, and your face suddenly looming over us in the moonlight. *If this is what I have for a sister*, you said, *I don't want it*. But I couldn't stand for you to be mad at me even overnight and pestered you with tearful mea culpas until forgiveness was mine.

Part of what stuck us together was the whole conspiracy of adolescent rebellion. It was us against our parents, our school, the authorities, the uncool adult world in general. Every few weeks, we pooled our allowance to buy twenty-dollar ounces of pot. I usually made the purchase, but only you could roll. Cross-legged on your white lacquer dresser, we carefully blew our smoke out the cracked-open window of your bedroom, then fumigated with pine-scented air freshener. I'm sure our parents were really bamboozled by a room that smelled like a reggae party in a gas station rest room.

High, we struck a perfect pitch of hilarity in each other. We could giggle for hours about nothing: some foible of our teachers or friends, the way a word starts to sound if you say it ten or twenty times. Our many obscure in-jokes were so profoundly silly that we could barely use certain phrases in each other's presence without wetting our pants. Don't you remember that one crazy game where the object was to make up a story that ended with the sentence "And then she saw the bottle of glue on the table"? Even years later, when I came up from college to visit you in your dorm at boarding school, I pointed to a bottle of Elmer's on the desk and repeated our famous punch line. We were rolling on the floor the rest of the weekend. God, I miss that.

Until well into our twenties, the basic rule held: any experience, any relationship, could and should be shared. So although heroin started off as your little secret with your boyfriend Steven, I wasn't about to be left out for long. We had that apartment in the city, the three of us, and a few nights a week we'd drive down after work in my old junker car, our stomachs doing somersaults while we discussed whether to buy one bag each or maybe four to split three ways. After lining up on the graffiti-covered stoops to buy our glassine packets and our needles, we'd race back home over the potholes on Fourteenth Street and turn on the dance music radio station all the way loud, and you would pull out your lucky belt from the bottom of your purse. Jump, jump, jump, to it, sang Aretha. Just as I could never roll joints, I could never shoot up either; you always had to do me after you did yours. Once we were high, we'd clean the house, make long-distance phone calls, play Jotto, and draw pictures with colored pencils, or sometimes go out to the Roxy and mingle with break-dancers.

Of course it wasn't always that easy, and it was never safe. There were nights we were sold packets of talcum powder, nights we were robbed outright, several nights we almost got busted, and one time we did. There were people who pretended to be our friends until they found the perfect moment to cheat us and disappear. And though most of the time we shared our drugs the same way we once split our Tabs, sometimes we even tried to cheat each other. Like that night before your wedding, when you took my coke and refilled the tinfoil packet with baking soda. You broke down and confessed just as I was tapping the white powder into a spoon. Then you went up on the roof and stayed there all night, doing the drugs we had stocked up for the reception.

When I got so high at work that my boss had to take me home on the subway, when I got beaten up and robbed trying to cop at four in the morning, when I spent an entire vacation in Montreal trying to force a reformed junkie friend to get me some drugs, I finally scared myself badly enough to move to a town where I had no dope connections. It was sheer luck and not for lack of trying that I never found any. When I left the city, Nancy, I honestly thought you would be all right. You and Steven seemed to have it under control. You would go on, I believed, getting high a few evenings a week, the way other people have a couple of beers. You had each other. Though after I left, that seemed to be all you had.

It took me a long time to realize how bad things were. Though we talked on the phone every week, you told me only what you wanted me to know. Of course, you were trying to quit. That was good enough. I didn't start to think otherwise until I came up to visit when I was pregnant, and for the first time I watched what was going on instead of participating. We hadn't seen each other in months, and yet that time you spent locked in the bathroom was the most important thing.

After that visit I'd ask every time we talked: *Have you guys been down?* Meaning: Did you buy drugs? But now I can see I half-wanted you to say yes, that some sick part of me didn't want my sister to stop shooting heroin. Why? Because you were my last connection? Because I refused to believe in the fact of addiction? Or was I still competing for the prize of Best Child? Was it that old-time schadenfreude spirit—I really didn't want your life to be okay?

I helped you rationalize your habit even while encouraging you to stop. And in the end—addicted bone-deep, crazy, spending close to a hundred bucks a day—you found the strength to save yourself without my help. You left Steven, checked into a rehab, joined Narcotics Anonymous, threw yourself into the Twelve Steps with zeal. Now you go to meetings every day, retreats on the weekends. You make speeches at the regional conferences. Your phone is always busy. You have friends

I've never met; you tell them a version of this story I don't know.

And there are many versions. A couple of years ago in New York I ran into my first boyfriend, you remember Jon, still gentle and funny and husky-voiced under the messy brown curls. He told me that he had read a piece I wrote, "Suburban Teens on Acid," and was disturbed by the lighthearted tone. He reminded me that at one of the very parties I had written about, Rosie Pinella had a bad trip, a raw hysterical breakdown, and we spent half the night terrified, trying to bring her back. He said that all those drugs we did cut his childhood too short, that we were pushed into situations we should never have had to confront. He said it ended up taking him an extra ten years to become an adult.

But we are all adults now, aren't we, and have our busy adult lives. Even when I go home to Mommy's for a visit, you don't have time to make the trip from North Jersey. I can't, you finally admitted. I don't want to feel the way I used to feel.

So what do I do? I drink gin with our mother and my husband while my kids sleep down the hall in your old room.

Do you remember a couple of months ago you told me the story of your friend from N.A.? When she was twenty-five her parents finally told her she had had a twin, a boy. A few days after their fifth birthday, the two of them were playing in the front yard when a drunk driver swerved out of control, jumped the curb, and killed her brother. Though she was unhurt, she didn't say a single word for almost a year. When she spoke again, she didn't ask about him, never uttered his name. So the parents followed suit; it seemed the right thing to do. Then the only thing to do. They hid the photographs, the monogrammed spoon.

All her life, you told me, she had the feeling that a part of her wasn't there. At least now she knows it's true. She knows his name.

You know, Nance, the word "sibling" comes from *sib*, "related by blood," and *-ling*, a diminutive suffix, as in "princeling." As in my little kin, my tribespuppy, my clansmuffin. My sibyl, my changeling, my sibilant darling girl. Once we shared a setting, a cast of characters, a hundred plots. Do we now share nothing, do we now go on as cameos in each other's lives? The two-in-one, the Siamese twins joined at the ego, don't you see they are gone? *We* is the name of the part of us that isn't here.

You held the scalpel and performed the surgery yourself. To save (I think you would say) your own life.

I could be letting myself off too easy, but I wonder if there isn't some kind of genetically encoded script being played out here. If there is, the sequel is already in production in my own kitchen, where just today the boys were whining for graham crackers. Well, the big one was actually saying "graham cracker," and the baby was standing beside him, whimpering supportively. I went to the cabinet, got the crackers, handed them around.

Seconds after I turned away, Big Brother had devoured his and snatched the other from the baby's unsuspecting hand. I heard a cry of infant outrage and wheeled back into the room in a fury. I scooped up Vincie, smacked Hayes harder than necessary, and grabbed the stolen cracker, shouting, You can't do this to him! You can't always take everything. For God's sake, let him have something for once! Let him have it, I said. Let go!

It's okay, honey, I told the baby, putting him down with his cracker. Eyes on his tearful sibling, he licked the cracker once, then handed it over.

Do the Night Thing

am standing in front of the window, almost repiercing my ears in a hasty attempt to get a pair of hoops through them, when I see the headlights of the babysitter's car slide up and flick off in front of the house. She's here, I call to Tony in the bathroom.

I answer the door in a tight black dress and lots of mascara. You'll be late, the babysitter concludes, surveying my appearance.

Probably, I agree, tossing back the last of my rum and Diet Coke. We kiss the kids good-bye, shouting pointless edicts about cookies and bedtime from the driveway. Then Tony starts the car, lights a cigarette, and heads downtown.

Not that I am a homebody by any stretch, but when it comes to nightclubs, I can honestly say We Hardly Go Out Anymore. The hours are too late, the people are too young, the drinks are too weak, the music is too loud; or maybe it's just us, having to get up and dole out the Cheerios at six-thirty every morning. But I've been hearing rumors about this new dance club in the warehouse district where the deejay is great and the dance floor is hot and the crowd is gay and straight and white and black and brown and I have to see for myself.

Even at my advanced stage in life, the thought of being in a place where all different kinds and colors of people party together is irresistible to me. Hip to hip, shoulder to shoulder, glass to glass with strangers from distant reaches of the social structure: that is where I feel the groove thang happen. One nation, under funk, with dollar drinks and strobe lights for all.

I'm talking about every club I've ever loved. Like the El Moroccan Room of my high school days in Asbury Park, New Jersey, a seventies gay disco with pink spotlights and feather boas, where several Diana Rosses tangoed with several Carol Channings while Tallulah Bankhead reapplied her lipstick and lip-synched Donna Summer. I don't think teenage girls in Earth Shoes were the El Moroccan's preferred clientele, but somehow we had the fake IDs and the right connections. A few years later, I headed out West and found the Bluebird in Fort Worth, Texas, a predominantly black blues shack where anybody with a bootie to shake could get herself in a peck of dance trouble in under five minutes. And the Split Rail in Austin, where hippies and Hell's Angels and cowboys coexisted in amiable drunkenness, gradually assimilating one another's hairstyles and dance steps. Just across town lay the Hollywood, where tough girls abruptly set down their drinks and their pool cues, tore off their T-shirts and tore up the dance floor, overcome by Saturday night fever.

When I moved back to New York, it was the Roxy, a roller rink turned nightclub at the peak of the breakdance era, the early rap days of Grandmaster Flash and the Rockers' Revenge. Behind the velvet rope a tangled mass of break-dancers from the boroughs and scenesters from downtown preened to get in. I had a crush on a barely teenage breaker in a red-and-green knitted ski cap; one night I screwed up the nerve to buy him a soda.

The gay bars of New Orleans's French Quarter in the early eighties, the Parade, the Bistro, the Loading Zone, the neon-lit high-wax dance floor where I first twirled with my own true love, the campy overdressed underdressed everybody in the doorless stalls of the bisexual bathroom making out, fixing up, getting down. The Tea Dance, the Beer Bust, the Two for One, the One for All, the videos, the bartenders, the Pointer Sisters. The wraparound balconies high above the tourists, far beneath the sky lit up with stars tiny and swooping like reflections from a mirror ball. Oh, girl.

And what about that place in San Francisco, that psychedelic block party of a bar, where massive straight men in muscle shirts danced inches away from their exquisitely coiffed gay cousins, where a ragtag dance crew of white and Latina women performed synchronized routines on stage and on video screens, where a whole contingent of Extremely Short Lesbians in Baseball Caps arrived en masse, where there were cool clothes and cutoffs and fat people and skinny people and just plain vanilla couples like me and Tony, if you can call us that. Short on attitude, long on dance mania. You put your drink down on somebody else's table and they actually smile.

That's all I want from a nightclub. Because there is something fundamentally lame about a roomful of white people dancing to black music. Because gay men invented nightlife as we know it. Because the more different kinds of people there are getting down, the hotter and bluer burns the party fire.

So we're not all the same. So what. Let's dance.

By now we've paid our cover and bought our kamikazes and are edging toward the gauze-draped dance floor to check it out. Three kids in high-top sneakers are doing a line dance to a rap song; a crowd of guys in Bermuda shorts and eyeliner casually watches them. A black man in a white shirt asks a white woman in a black dress to dance, and she moves toward him, smiling. Behind me, a couple of Asian girls are talking about Jell-O shots. No Jell-O shots tonight, one states definitively. That's on Tuesdays. Then some hot new song comes on and the dance floor fills up. Tony starts to move in that effortless foot-sliding way he has, as if he were distantly related to Michael Jackson. Come on, he mouths, beginning to disappear among the bodies and lights, and I do.

I think the babysitter was right. We're going to be late.